ALWAYS

AND IN

EVERYTHING

DISCOVER THE LIFE-CHANGING POWER
OF GIVING THANKS IN ALL THINGS

GABRIEL CLEATOR

TABLE OF CONTENTS

———

DEDICATION

I want to dedicate this book to
my Mom and Dad,
Betty and Jeff Cleator

To my Mom,
for her unmatched example of exhibiting
the joy of our Lord to us

To my Dad,
whose love for the truth of the Scriptures
instilled in me that same love

I am grateful for you!

ACKNOWLEDGEMENTS

WRITING A BOOK is a large undertaking that requires a team effort. Honestly, I am not a natural writer. Speaking the truth is much easier for me than sharing it in writing. This book would not have come to pass without the hard work and dedication of those that helped me edit it.

First, I want to thank my wonderful wife Sara! Without her loving support and tireless work editing this volume, you would not be reading this book today.

I also want to thank my sister Bethany. In the early stages of writing this book, I struggled to make the paragraphs and chapters flow together smoothly, since writing is not my strong point. My sister, on the other hand, is a great creative writer and she patiently worked through the entire book, spending hours reworking sentences and content to make it flow better, and provided some wonderful insights of her own. Her love for the Lord and knowledge of writing made her invaluable in preparing this book.

I want to express my gratitude to Dr. and Mrs. D, whose continued encouragement to saturate my life in the Word and to share the truth of giving thanks with others is a wonderful blessing to me.

Thank you also to Ross and Jonathan for their willingness to read through this document in its early stages and provide comments and edits. Their input was another key part in this process of preparing this book.

My parents, to whom this book is dedicated, also deserve a huge thank you as their encouraging words and attitudes helped spur me on in the writing of this volume.

I want to express my gratitude for my sister-in-law Erika Mathews who is a professional editor but graciously did a final edit on this manuscript for me as a gift.

A big thank you also goes to Zyrek Castelino for his great work in designing the cover for this book. I appreciate his professional design skills, his attention to detail, and all the time he put into creating this cover for me.

Even though my name is on the cover as the author, this book is the work of a whole team. I could share the names of countless others who have had an impact on my life, and therefore in some way or another played a part in the making of this book. May the Lord richly bless each of you who helped with this publication in some measure for how you have blessed me. This book would not be here without you!

Most of all, I want to give thanks to my Lord and Savior Jesus Christ! I am so thankful for His salvation and for the forming of His life in me. I am unspeakably grateful to God for the precious gift of His Word, the Bible, which reveals His heart that we would walk as His thankful and rejoicing people who express His life to a dying world that desperately needs it. Thank you, Lord!

WHY A BOOK ON GIVING THANKS

HAVE YOU EVER noticed a discrepancy between the description of the Christian life that we read in the Bible and what we see around us in other Christians—and even ourselves? Have you wondered, in light of verses like Romans 8:37 that share that we are more than conquerors through Christ, why so many professing believers appear to be living in defeat? Maybe you have read 1 Peter 1:8 where the Scripture talks about us having joy unspeakable and being full of glory, and pondered why, if this is indeed true, so many followers of Christ suffer from discouragement. Have you reflected on the fact that the Scriptures say that the joy of the Lord is our strength (see Nehemiah 8:10) and wondered why so many Christians seem to complain and lack joy?

If we look first at the picture God gives us in His Word of a normal Christian, one who lives an overcoming and rejoicing life, and then at the Christian world around us, we have to be struck by the fact that we do not really look like the picture. Does that bother you? It certainly bothers me. It would not bother me as much if I only saw it in other people; what bothers me the most are the discrepancies in me. You may notice that when one finger is pointing at all those "other" Christians, three fingers indeed point in a convicting way in the direction of the one doing the pointing.

If God says that a Christian is one who lives a joyful, overcoming, victorious life, then this type of life must be accessible to us! According to the Scriptures, not only is this victorious life available to us, but it should be normal for us as believers. In light of this, the questions we must ask are: How do we begin to live and walk in this "more than conqueror," dynamic, rejoicing life that God calls us to? What are we missing that keeps us from living and walking in the reality of what "normal" Christianity is supposed to look like?

I believe that one of the keys to living the joyful Christianity the New Testament talks about is what I would like to share with you in this book. This concept is presented in Scripture time and time again, yet we often miss its life-changing significance. This truth touches literally every area of life and is very close to the heart of God. Sometimes, violating this principle is excused by calling it "not that big of a deal," but some of God's harshest judgments in Scripture come on those who violate it.

Some of the discrepancies in our lives that were mentioned earlier come from disobeying this command. Living out this truth has the potential of revolutionizing your relationship with the Lord and deepening it in a way that you may have not even known was possible.

The truth I am talking about is the life-changing power of giving thanks in everything. Maybe you are thinking, "Is that all, just giving thanks?" If that thought came to your mind, you may be in for a surprise. This command to give thanks has more weight and implications for our lives than many of us have imagined. Beginning to walk in this truth has the potential to radically affect your whole life like it still does to mine.

Before we delve into this truth, we have to allow the Lord to cut to the very core of our belief system to something that greatly hinders us from giving thanks in everything. If we were perfectly honest, we may have to admit that, deep down in our hearts, we believe life is about us and our happiness. We believe that God's goal is to make us happy.

This belief is demonstrated when we believe either that God is trying to make us happy today—in this life—with health, wealth, and wisdom, or thinking that although we struggle along in this life, one day God will make us happy in heaven. We need to see that we have wrongly believed that God is about us; the truth is that we were created for Him.

Stop and think about it. The belief that God exists to make us happy leads us to pursue God with the goal of personal happiness. Sometimes Christian books and messages will say something like this: Living for yourself and living in sin will ultimately lead to a life of sadness and unfulfillment. Come to Jesus and He will make you happy and give you fulfillment and joy.

Do you see that the objective of this philosophy is ultimately personal happiness? This is no more than a Christian brand of humanism. Honestly, at times I have been guilty of this "Christian humanism," thinking that God was about me and my personal happiness, instead of believing the truth that life is about God and His glory.

What does all this have to do with giving thanks? If I enter a relationship with the Lord, believing that life is primarily about me, I will have a self-centered outlook.

Inevitably, throughout life things do not go our way, and our false ideas about the purpose of the Christian life cause us to murmur and complain. Whether or not we realize it, when we complain, we are speaking against the Lord for not causing things to work how we wanted. Instead of being the thankful people that God has called us to be, our lives end up being marked by complaining and whining that life did turn out as jolly as we hoped it would as we followed God.

Whenever I visit a Christian bookstore, I am always struck by the sheer amount of books and music that all scream at you that life is about you being fulfilled and happy, and God is all about you and your personal needs. I now want to tell you something that we rarely ever hear: life is not about you. Life is not about me. Life is about God.

If you are looking for a book that is going to tell you how to pursue your dreams and be all that you want to be, you have picked up the wrong book. One reason we murmur and complain so often is because our plans have not worked out, our dreams have been shattered, and life has spiraled out of our control. We feel our only recourse is to verbalize our dissatisfaction. Our frustration and disillusionment with life is often founded on the faulty belief system that God is about us. Praise God for the glorious, liberating truth that life is not about us. What a salvation it is when God delivers us from living for ourselves to instead live unto Him!

Since life is about God, not me, I can give thanks for everything He causes or allows in my life, knowing that He is working it out for His good purpose as I love Him and seek His face.

Please do not misunderstand me. God deeply loves us and cares about us. He tenderly watches over us His sheep as a good Shepherd and comforts us as a good Father cares for His children. Actually, God loves us so much that He delivers us from living for ourselves and brings us into the glorious life of living for the One Who created us, who is HIMSELF!

This book is a call to all believers to surrender ourselves to God's will for our lives by choosing, through the power of Christ Himself, to give thanks in everything. I want to look at numerous testimonies in Scripture that speak about giving thanks, share with you personal testimonies of how this principle of gratefulness has changed my life, and look at a few stories from believers who have gone before us. I want to look at how we can walk in this truth every day and how it affects every area of our lives. Let me assure you that if you begin to surrender to God's will for your life by walking in gratefulness to the Lord each day, your life will never be the same.

CHAPTER ONE

WHAT IS GOD'S WILL FOR YOUR LIFE?

MY JOURNEY IN the discovery of this truth began quietly, without fanfare. I was in my late teens and God was really working in my life. I was beginning to learn the importance of spending time reading and meditating on the Word of God, and I was seeing God changing my life in the process!

One fall day I flew into the Chicago O'Hare airport. I had a little extra time while I was waiting for my ride, so I opened my pocket New Testament and began to read. The verses I read that chilly November evening were destined to change my life. This is what I read:

> This know also, that in the last days perilous times shall come. For men shall be lovers of their own selves, covetous, boasters, proud, blasphemers, disobedient to parents, **unthankful**, unholy. (2 Timothy 3:1–2, emphasis added)

The word *unthankful* seemed to jump off the page at me! I stopped as the Lord opened my eyes to see that *the Lord placed unthankfulness in the same list as unholiness!* Truthfully, before this when I had thought about ungratefulness, I thought of it mostly as being unpleasant, and that God would rather us be thankful and not complain. I had never before considered unthankfulness to be as serious as unholiness! Since God included both of these sins on the same list, ungratefulness must be more serious than I had realized. I made a mental note to look further into God's Word and see what it had to say about the seriousness of unthankfulness and of the importance of giving thanks.

Little did I know that God was going to show me a theme that runs throughout the whole Bible: that God is inviting us to continuous fellowship with Him through thanksgiving.

Later, after this discovery at the airport, I opened a Bible program on my computer and searched for verses on giving thanks. The Scriptures that appeared on the screen were like a treasure chest overflowing with nuggets; I saw treasures of God's truth that confirmed the idea that God had planted in my heart earlier—that thankfulness is incredibly important to God and therefore essential to my relationship with Him and the fulfillment of His purpose for my life.

One of those nuggets is 1 Thessalonians 5:18:

> In every thing give thanks: for this is the will of God in Christ Jesus concerning you.

This verse struck me in a new way. It does not just command us to give thanks, but states that giving thanks actually plays a key part in God's will for our lives. A question I wrestled with and have heard so many people ask is, "What is God's will for my life?" Particularly, young people are apt to ask this as they see life spread out before them and wonder what God has planned for them. In fact, does not everyone, young or old, wonder the same thing? When I have the opportunity to speak different places, sometimes I will ask the audience how many of them are wondering or have wondered what God's will for their life is, and many hands always go up. This question is a common one, but perhaps the answer is different than we might think.

I already touched on the answer to this nagging question when I mentioned that we were created for God and not for ourselves, but in 1 Thessalonians 5:18, God makes it clear that His will for us is inseparably connected to *giving thanks in everything.* This is not what we had in mind when we asked the question! We wanted to know what state God wants us to live in, who He wants us to marry, or what job He wants us to apply for. These are good questions, but they often spring from a misconception. We are quick to assume that God's will for our lives is something in the future. Certainly, God has plans for our future, but what about today? Scripture says that we are not to take thought for, or to be anxious about, tomorrow. So instead of worrying about the future, perhaps we should be asking God what His will is for us to live and to walk in right now. We do not have far to go for the answer to that question. Our gracious Father has already given us a delightful command, a stirring rally cry: *"In everything give thanks."* God wants to lead and guide us in all areas of our lives, but we need to remember that, throughout all things that come across our paths, His overarching desire is that we give thanks to Him.

Instead of worrying and wondering about the future, we need to focus on what God has to say about His will for us. We have to be careful that we don't get so caught up trying to figure out our future that we miss God in the present!

Am I saying that the totality of God's will for our lives is giving thanks? Maybe you are thinking, "I can see how thanksgiving is important, but isn't there more to God's will for my life than just the giving of thanks?" God's will is so much bigger than just the life decisions like who to marry and what career to pursue. Although, as was mentioned, God wants to lead us in these vital areas, He has an even larger goal in mind that is bigger than just our individual lives. God wants to purify us as a holy people that He can build together as His sacred habitation. (See Ephesians 2:22.) Part of the way He accomplishes this is by conforming us to the image of His Son and cleansing us as vessels into which He can form His life. How does God accomplish His desire of making us sanctified channels for His use? Often it is through trials and irritations. God wants to use the difficulties we walk through to burn off the dross in our lives and shape us into His image.

If God's will is indeed to shape us into His likeness and fill us with Himself, and if He uses trials to do this, then it is vitally important that we receive those hardships with thanksgiving. If we reject the trials with murmuring and complaining, we unwittingly miss out on the eternal work that God wants to do in and through them, and so resist His will. This is why it is vitally important that we receive everything with thanksgiving, which opens the door for God to use everything in our lives to mold us into His image and fill us with Himself—and in so doing, fulfill His will for us.

We were created for God's pleasure, not our pleasure, and giving thanks in everything is a significant part of bringing God glory and pleasure through our lives and accomplishing His will. Romans 11:36 puts it this way, *"For of him, and through him, and to him, are all things: to whom be glory for ever. Amen."*

All things are for HIM. We were created for Him, we were saved for Him, and we live for Him and His purpose! Everything that was made has a purpose, and things function best when they are used for the purpose they were created for. Can openers, for example, were created for opening cans. Maybe you could use a can opener to dig a hole, but that would be very difficult because that was not what can openers were designed for. They are best suited to be used for the purpose they were created for: to open cans.

You and I were created for the pleasure and purpose of God. We see in Revelation 4:11 that everything, including ourselves, was created for God's pleasure: *"Thou art worthy, O Lord, to receive glory and honour and power: for thou hast created all things, and for thy pleasure they are and were created."* Just like can openers were not made for digging holes, we were not made for our pleasure. When we try to live life with our personal happiness as our end goal, we end up murmuring and complaining when life turns out different than we planned because we were not created to live for ourselves.

Romans 8:28 says, *"And we know that all things work together for good to them that love God, to them who are the called according to his purpose."* This well-known verse seems to be often misunderstood and misused, in part because in our minds we have equated God working all things together for good with God working all things together for our personal happiness. The reality is that God working all things together for good is *not* Him working all things together primarily to make us happy, but rather Him working all things together for the accomplishment of His purpose.

I am most usable to God when I am fully submitted to Him to use for the reason for which I was made: to bring Him pleasure and be used by Him for His purpose. Giving thanks is a practical way to acknowledge the reality that life is about the pleasure and glory of God.

We need to realize that God's will for our lives is greater than our physical existence or personal experiences. God has more for us than simply pursuing a career, being involved in a ministry, or raising a family. God's will for us is intertwined with *Himself*. A big part of God's will for our lives is that He be recognized in us; the very life of the Lord Jesus Himself is to be seen in who we are as His created beings. One of the things that God takes great delight in and that causes Him to be seen in our lives is thanksgiving.

> So we thy people and sheep of thy pasture will **give thee thanks for ever:** we will shew forth thy praise to all generations. (Psalm 79:13, emphasis added)

Giving thanks in everything is a practical, day by day demonstration of the life of God within us, because it is through Him and to Him that we give thanks. It is something that we do by His grace that brings Him pleasure. The answer to these two weighty questions, "Why was I created?" and "What is God's will for my life?" is intertwined with giving thanks to God.

The incredible discovery of the power of giving thanks did not end in a Chicago airport, nor did this discovery climax with a word search. It began spreading into every area of my life. When God begins to teach us something, He will often bring us opportunities to put it into practice. Not long after the Lord first began teaching me about the power of giving thanks, He allowed me to be tested.

I was helping load a large box into the back of a pickup truck. The box was long and seemed to stick out a bit too far. I was not sure if the tailgate of the truck would be able to close. The guy I was working with reached forward, grasped the tailgate, and prepared to slam it, hoping it would somehow shut. My friend did not realize that my hand was sitting on the edge of the truck, right in the way of the tailgate. Smash! He slammed the tailgate…right onto my finger! The tailgate clicked so securely into place that my finger became stuck between the truck and its tailgate. Two thoughts came rushing to my brain at once. The first thought was simple and predictable: *"That hurt!"* The second thought was also simple, but completely opposed to my natural tendencies. It came clear as a bell and resonated within me: *"In everything give thanks."* My finger being smashed was part of everything. So in spite of how I felt, I began to thank and praise the Lord for the pain that was shooting through my finger. I rejoiced as I opened that tailgate and pulled out my smashed finger.

Something astonishing happened as I thanked the Lord. This situation, which could have simply been an irritating, painful experience, became a wonderful time of joy and fellowship with my Savior as I thanked Him.

God has allowed many different situations in my life to teach me something incredible: *that every irritation becomes an invitation to enter into the presence of the Lord when we receive it with thanksgiving.* We need to see that in every irritation and trial, God bids us to enter into His presence with thanksgiving, because even they are a part of everything.

Irritations are going to come into our lives no matter what. Even if our fingers are never slammed in a tailgate, we all are going to experience difficulties. Trials are not a matter of "if," but of "when." However, the reality of impending trials is not a discouraging prospect if we remember that all trials and irritations are part of everything. They are opportunities to see the will of our Heavenly Father fulfilled in our lives. They are occasions to give thanks.

When we are faced with difficulties, we have two choices. One choice is to resist the trial by grumbling and complaining. The consequences of that choice are that we become angry and bitter and our lives get destroyed. The other option is to receive the trial with thanksgiving as an invitation from the Lord to enter into His presence. If we do that, we will see the Lord use the trial or irritation to conform us to the image of His Son, and we find that God's will is being fulfilled through us just as we longed for it to be. Giving thanks in everything, through the power of Christ in us, can mean that the trial we are facing can become something that God can use powerfully in our lives to accomplish His purpose.

Another time God gave me an invitation to give thanks in otherwise irritating circumstances was when I was in central Texas. I enjoy photography, so I eagerly grabbed my camera and headed outside to get some nature shots. I stopped in one spot for a few moments and raised my camera, pausing to position it just so in order to get the shot I wanted. All at once, I felt a stinging pain in my hand. A fire ant had ventured up my leg to my hand and stung me. I looked down and, to my horror, realized that my pant leg was crawling with fire ants! Unknowingly, I had stepped right into a fire ant mound! I leaped away and began to hop around, wildly knocking the fire ants off my pant leg. This was an irritating situation, and my natural response would be to complain and grumble. Instead, right as I felt the sting of the bite, the Lord in His mercy reminded me what my duty was: to give thanks. After all, having my leg swarming with fire ants is part of everything! As I swatted frantically, I began to rejoice and praise the Lord. I was taking God up on the invitation He had given me to come before His presence with thanksgiving. As I did so, something incredible happened. Instead of feeling anger and irritation, the Lord filled me with His joy! In fact, I was actually able to laugh at how funny I must have looked hopping around, frantically slapping myself. Thankfully, I only got one or two ant bites!

Trials and tests are going to come into our lives no matter what. Some of those trials are small, like getting attacked by a nest of fire ants, while others are much more serious, like losing a job or being diagnosed with a dangerous disease. No matter what, the trials are going to come. We can either resist the test or trial by complaining, or receive the trial or test with thanksgiving. In this way, trials can become opportunities to enter the Lord's presence. Through giving thanks in all things, we are able to not merely endure trials, but triumph in them and see them become glorious times of fellowship with God. The question is whether or not we will say "yes" to God's command to give thanks in all things. Will we say "yes" to His invitation to enter His presence?

We are to come before the presence of the Lord with thanksgiving. *"Let us come before his presence with thanksgiving, and make a joyful noise unto him with psalms"* (Psalm 95:2).

The Lord began making it clearer and clearer to me that applying this principle of giving thanks in all things is key to continuous fellowship with Him. He began to apply this principle to every part of my life. As a result, I was brought into a more conscious, continuous abiding in the Lord's presence. Situations that once worried or irritated me were transformed into doorways of glorious opportunity to apply this principle of giving thanks in everything and to experience the presence and power of God in an entirely new way!

God's will includes us knowing Him and Him knowing us. His will is not limited to tomorrow. His will is for us to walk in a personal, abiding relationship with Him today. Thanksgiving is a huge key to walking in that oneness with Him. Little wonder that God places unthankfulness on the same list with unholiness! A lack of thankfulness hinders the pleasure of our Creator from being fulfilled in our lives; giving thanks, on the other hand, is part of walking in an intimate knowing of God on a daily basis, and it brings Him great pleasure.

David makes a powerful statement in Psalm 6:4–5: *"Return, O Lord, deliver my soul: oh save me for thy mercies' sake. For in death there is no remembrance of thee: in the grave who shall give thee thanks?"* In Psalm 30:9, he also says, *"What profit is there in my blood, when I go down to the pit? Shall the dust praise thee? shall it declare thy truth?"*

One of David's reasons for living was to give thanks and praise to the Lord. Can you and I say the same? Are we so surrendered to the will of God that one motivation for us to get up in the morning is so that we might thank and praise the Lord as He has commanded us to? Even David's desire for the Lord's deliverance was so that he could thank Him! Giving thanks to the Lord and praising Him are causes worth living for because they are part of walking in oneness with Him.

Giving thanks is an incredibly powerful action that will revolutionize your walk with the Lord. God desires that we begin to fulfill His will for our life and bring pleasure to Him, our Creator, by walking in a personal relationship with Him. This is our high calling. This is our created purpose.

CHAPTER TWO

THE SIN WE EXCUSE

BEFORE WE DELVE any deeper into our exploration of thanksgiving, we need to take a look at a sin that is the exact opposite of giving thanks. Many of us do this without realizing that it is sin! It is probably one of the most excused sins that creep into our lives. If we are going to delve deeper into the riches and power of giving thanks, light must be shed on this sin, because it hinders us from fulfilling God's will and from abiding continuously in the presence of the Lord. As it is exposed and cleansed by the power of Christ, we will experience a new freedom and a greater power than ever before.

The sin I am referring to is the sin of complaining. If we stop and pay close attention to our conversations throughout the day, we may be surprised to discover how often complaining is heard from our lips or is unspoken but is in our hearts. Sadly, while we claim to seek God's will, our lives are often cluttered with the very complaining that keeps us from it.

In the Biblical account of the children of Israel, we see that a lack of thankfulness hinders God's purpose for our lives. God's will for the children of Israel when He brought them out Egypt was that they enter the Promised Land. Since the children of Israel chose to complain instead of to give thanks, they were kept out of the Promised Land. Just as the children of Israel were unable to enter into it because of their complaining, you and I may not fulfill God's will for our lives in the future unless we fulfill God's will for our lives in the present by giving thanks in all things.

Complaining is speaking against the Lord. We read in God's Word about how the children of Israel were brought out of Egypt, out of the bondage to their enemies, and how they began a journey to the Promised Land in fulfillment of God's will for them. Yet they were not allowed to enter that land. Why not? Why did God's judgment come upon them so many times as they traveled in the wilderness? One of the biggest reasons was that they were ungrateful; the children of Israel brought judgment on themselves because they complained.

Numbers 11 describes how the people of Israel complained while they were in the wilderness. Listen to the swift judgment that came upon the people of Israel because of the complaining that flowed from their ungrateful hearts:

> And when the people complained, it displeased the LORD: and the LORD heard it; and his anger was kindled and the fire of the LORD burnt among them, and consumed them that were in the uttermost parts of the camp.

One would imagine that after experiencing such swift judgment from the Lord, they would have repented of their ungratefulness and stopped complaining! However, if we read further in the chapter, we hear the people complaining again. Numbers 11:4–5 says:

> And the mixt multitude that was among them fell a lusting: and the children of Israel also wept again, and said, Who shall give us flesh to eat? We remember the fish, which we did eat in Egypt freely; the cucumbers, and the melons, and the leeks, and the onions, and the garlick:

God provided for all of the needs of His people. He supernaturally supplied manna for them to eat and did not allow their clothes or shoes to wear out. (See Deuteronomy 29:5.) He gave them deliverance from Egypt and guided them throughout their journey to their new home. Yet despite all of these amazing mercies of God, the people, in rebellion, complained and said that they wanted meat. We see the seriousness of this complaining in verse 20. Listen to what the Lord says in response to the complaining of His people:

> …because that **ye have despised the LORD** which is among you, and have wept before him, saying, Why came we forth out of Egypt? (emphasis added)

This is why complaining is so serious. The Lord has a very sobering definition of complaining that helps us understand why it is so grievous to Him and why He brings such swift and severe judgment against those who complain. *In God's estimation, complaining is despising Him.* When we complain, we are saying that His provision as our Heavenly Father is inadequate, and therefore we are speaking against Him. Our culture may excuse complaining, other believers might accept complaining as justifiable, and we may even be tempted to tolerate it in our own lives, but that does not change the truth that our God does not excuse complaining. He does not let it slip by unaddressed.

How is complaining actually speaking against the Lord? This illustration may help explain it. Imagine meeting a young boy, and he describes to you what his life at home is like. You know that his parents are good people who have his best interest in mind. Imagine that this young boy tells you that he has very few toys and does not have time for having fun. Then he continues by saying that he does not like the food he eats at home, and there are activities and possessions that he wants, but is not allowed to have. You might walk away from that conversation starting to think that the boy's parents are not very good parents after all. Even if the boy did not mention his parents, you still might draw negative conclusions about them because of his words. Maybe the parents were doing what was best for the boy by withholding things from his life that they knew would harm him. Maybe he had dietary needs that he did not understand, so to benefit his health, his parents had him avoid foods he liked. Maybe they required him to work hard to excel in areas they knew would benefit him later in life but which he found to be boring. Yet, because he spoke against the actions of his parents, he spoke against his parents and misrepresented them. Since we are children of our Heavenly Father, when we murmur and complain about what He has caused or allowed, we speak against Him. We misrepresent our Father Who is perfect and does all things well. Complaining is slandering the name of our Heavenly Father.

When reading the account of the Lord delivering the children of Israel out of bondage and setting them free, it is easy for us to be critical of them and to wonder how they could so quickly begin to despise Him and complain. In listening to our everyday conversations, though, we have to realize that actually many believers, including myself, have done this as well! The Lord gloriously saved us from our sin by the death and resurrection of His Son. He brought us out of the bondage of darkness into His glorious light. He set us free just as He saved the children of Israel from Egypt. Yet, like the children of Israel, we are filled with ungratefulness and we complain. This is a grave sin that calls for repentance.

Scripture says that Satan is the accuser of the brethren. (See Revelation 12:10.) When we murmur and complain, we are agreeing with Satan, the accuser, in speaking against the Lord and others. In 1 Corinthians 10:10–11 we read, *"Neither murmur ye, as some of them also murmured, and were destroyed of the destroyer. Now all these things happened unto them for ensamples: and they are written for our admonition, upon whom the ends of the world are come."*

God warns us to look at examples like the one found in Numbers 11 about the seriousness of complaining and the swift judgment that fell upon the people that complained. We must take heed to the testimonies in God's Word that demonstrate the dire consequences of murmuring. I believe when we murmur and complain about difficult circumstances and people, we invite the enemy into those situations. We only have two choices when we face irritations and difficulties in life. We can invite the enemy into the situation through murmuring, or we can invite the Lord into the situation through giving thanks.

In 1 Corinthians 10, the word translated murmur means "to grumble." We hear and speak words of grumbling all too often. We constantly say things like, "It is so miserably hot outside today!" "This has been a horrible day," or "Nothing in my life ever turns out right!" Grumbling comes naturally to us. When we grumble, we tell God that His provision is inadequate for us. Our natural thought probably would not even identify grumbling as sin. Only as our Lord exposes our grumbling for what it is, speaking against Him, and only as we allow the power of His grace to overcome our complaining, will we experience the joy and power of gratefulness. Then we will see God's will fulfilled in our lives by giving thanks in everything. Let us take heed to the serious admonition on the danger of grumbling and complaining, lest we fall as the children of Israel did.

The Israelites were unable to enter the Promised Land because of their murmurings and grumblings. The Lord said of them:

> How long shall I bear with this evil congrega-
> tion, which murmur against me? I have heard the
> murmurings of the children of Israel, which they
> murmur against me. Say unto them, As truly as
> I live, saith the LORD, as ye have spoken in mine
> ears, so will I do to you: Your carcases shall fall in
> this wilderness; and all that were numbered of you,
> according to your whole number, from twenty
> years old and upward, which have murmured
> against me. (Numbers 14:27–29)

The Lord desired His people to enter the Promised Land. He longed for them to come to the peace, rest, and joy that was in store for them. He already declared that He would give them victory over their enemies. All they had to do was walk in the victory. God wanted to bless His people by giving them the land He promised as their inheritance, but instead of receiving these promises from the Lord, the people chose to reject the Lord's plan and they whined and complained. Our God does all things well. Even in trials and testings, He seeks to bring us deeper into a relationship with Him, into righteousness, peace, and joy. The grumbling and complaining that we are quick to overlook and even rationalize keeps us from seeing the promises and power of God in our lives. Victory over grumbling is vital for knowing a victorious life in Christ.

Why did the children of Israel complain? Why do you and I complain? Instead of looking to the Lord, the people of Israel looked at their circumstances and were fearful and discontent. As a result, their beliefs about their circumstances, and about the Lord, came out of their mouths. They grumbled because of what they believed. Therefore, they were unable to receive the countless blessings the Lord had in store for them. Just as God had already declared that His people could enjoy the Promised Land, He has made available to us a life of joy and hope, which is life with Christ Himself living in us.

The way of victory has already been opened up to us on the cross. God desires that we walk in the victory He has already won for us, just as the Promised Land was available to the children of Israel. He desires to bless us with all spiritual blessings. He desires that we enter into His promised peace, rest, and joy through giving thanks in all things. Our part is simple. Our delightful responsibility is to believe the truth about God—to believe that God is Who He says He is and that what He has promised He will do for us. However, instead of entering into our promised inheritance, like the children of Israel, we often turn our gaze upon our circumstances, thus taking it off of Jesus, and begin complaining. To murmur is to take our eyes off the Lord and put them on the situation; to give thanks is to take our eyes off the situation and put them on the Lord!

Just as the children of Israel saw only the hardship and battles they would face as they claimed their inheritance of the Promised Land, when you and I think about the trials and pain we are facing, we are tempted to complain. We doubt God's provision, promises, and power. We are kept from fulfilling God's good, acceptable, and perfect will for our lives, because instead of thanking Him, we complain. God's grace is sufficient for whatever trial or difficulty He allows in our lives. When we complain, we are resisting the Lord and His power, and therefore keeping ourselves from receiving the grace that will empower us to endure, and even triumph, through that difficulty. Giving thanks, on the other hand, is receiving the Lord's grace and humbling ourselves under His will. Humbling ourselves in obedience to God's clear command, "in everything give thanks," enables us to receive the available grace of God. We cannot afford to complain! We are desperately in need of the grace of God. We must begin believing the truth about Who our Lord is and speaking that truth in our heart and with our mouth instead of spewing out the "harmless" complaints that are actually not harmless at all.

Philippians 2:14 instructs us, *"Do all things without murmurings and disputings."* Everything we do must be done without murmuring or complaining. Does this include menial everyday tasks, like going to work day after day, washing dishes, and mowing the lawn? Absolutely! All too often we find ourselves murmuring about the "drudgery" of the tasks in daily life. God desires to renew our minds so we can see the seemingly mundane tasks as opportunities to fellowship with Him through giving thanks. No matter how difficult the task or how hard the trial, we are to do everything without murmuring. This requires a dramatic change in thinking! We are used to grumbling about countless things throughout the day. Sadly, complaining has become as habitual to us as small talk. We must stop and reevaluate our conversation and manner of life in all things. God has declared that a key part of His will for our lives is for us to give thanks in everything. If we desire His will to be a part of our everyday life, we must receive a life of thanksgiving instead of complaining.

This brings us to an important question: what does it look like to do all things without complaining? The life of Jesus Christ is the only life that does not complain. Christ in us is our hope for no longer living a life of complaining and speaking against God. *The key to deliverance from murmuring and complaining is humbly receiving the grace of God through giving thanks.* We cannot give thanks and murmur at the same time!

One of the reasons that the children of Israel did not enter the Promised Land was that they focused on the giants living there and became fearful. This focus resulted in complaining. Complaining and fear often go hand in hand because both involve a lack of focus on the Lord. When you and I are faced with "giants" such as fear and bitterness, often we are quick to give in to fear and verbally express a lack of faith in God and His promises. The opposite of complaining is giving thanks! Rejecting complaining and choosing to thank the Lord is a powerful way to humble ourselves and receive God's grace and victory.

Before the children of Israel entered the Promised Land or slew the giants that lived there, it was already theirs because God promised it to them; we have already been given victory in Christ over the "giants" of fear, bitterness, loneliness, and more, so we just need to receive with thanksgiving the victory we already have. Complaining is like choosing to stay behind in the wilderness instead of entering the Promised Land! Every day, regardless of the challenges that we face, God's will is for us to give thanks. As we turn our eyes upon Jesus and thank Him for the victory that He has already won, we will discover that God's promises are faithful.

Complaining keeps us wandering in the "wilderness" of depression, fear, and anxiety as we blame God, people, and circumstances for our difficulties. On the other hand, giving thanks in the midst of trials opens the way for us to receive the power of God and to triumph no matter what.

Are you wandering in the wilderness of depression? Are you walking through valleys fraught with trials and suffering? I urge you to enter the promised land of the joy of the Lord by giving thanks in all things. Your circumstances may not change immediately, and the trials may not vanish instantly. The valleys do not become mountains, but when we give thanks to the Lord, we will find that the valleys are God's training ground where He transforms us into His likeness by the power of the

Holy Spirit. Our Lord does not snatch us from the trial but gives us an invitation. Even while we are in the valley, we are invited to come before His presence through giving thanks. God's will for our lives may be accomplished in the darkest valley if we come before His presence with thanksgiving.

Did you know the world is engulfed in something akin to a life-threatening epidemic? Complaining is like an epidemic. It spreads swiftly, and even believers can get caught in this dangerous habit.

My first job after high school was at a fast-food restaurant. While I always got Sundays off, I cringed when my non-Christian coworkers described what working on Sundays was like. They told me that some of the hardest customers to deal with were the after-church crowd. Why? They had bad attitudes! What a poor testimony this was to my unbelieving coworkers. What were they to think when they saw those who claimed to be believers in the Savior and the children of a loving heavenly Father complaining and making life miserable for those around them?

As believers in Christ, we should be the most grateful people on earth! After all, the King we claim to serve has given us an unwavering mandate: "in everything give thanks." What is the world supposed to think when they see us disregarding His command and complaining? What conclusions are they going to draw about our God when we are constantly speaking against His working in our lives? Complaining has become a social norm; it is common to complain about weather, traffic, prices, politics, and just about everything else. We say, "God is so good!" and then turn around and speak against Him by complaining. Complaining in the lives of those who claim to be God's children is a sobering evidence of hypocrisy.

Complaining is not only a serious sin against God and a hindrance to our testimony before others, it also quenches the Spirit. 1 Thessalonians 5:16–19 says, *"Rejoice evermore. Pray without ceasing. In everything give thanks: for this is the will of God in Christ Jesus concerning you. Quench not the Spirit."* There seems to be a connection between the command to give thanks in all things and the instruction to not quench the Spirit. Similarly, Ephesians 4:30 instructs us to not grieve the Spirit. Few things grieve the Holy Spirit and quench His work in our lives more than murmuring and complaining. This is another reason that 2 Timothy 3:1–2 would place unthankfulness on the same plane as unholiness! I believe it keeps us from the fullness of God's Holy Spirit. As we are beginning to see more and more clearly, complaining is grievous to God and costs more than we realize.

It is not enough to merely stop complaining; our lives must be filled with thankfulness. A lack of thankfulness is a serious sin! One reason it is so serious is because it leads to vain imaginations, like Romans 1 talks about. *"Because that, when they knew God, they glorified him not as God, neither were thankful; but became vain in their imaginations, and their foolish heart was darkened"* (Romans 1:21).

The reason these men wandered away from God and had their hearts darkened, was that they glorified Him not as God *and were not thankful.* This lack of thankfulness was part of what led them to become vain in their imaginations. Romans 1 shows us a sequence of how a heart gets harder and harder and leads an ungrateful person to become an unmerciful,

THE SIN WE EXCUSE

backbiting hater of God. This whole horrible sequence began with not glorifying God as God and by being unthankful. A lack of thankfulness truly is a life-threatening condition!

Not giving thanks is one of the most prideful things we can do. A lack of thankfulness reveals that deep down in our hearts, even if we never say it out loud, we believe the lie that we have gained what we have by ourselves and in our own strength. We are not recognizing God and His position in our lives. In reality, everything that we have has been given to us by our gracious Heavenly Father. 1 Corinthians 4:7 says, *"For who maketh thee to differ from another? and what hast thou that thou didst not receive? now if thou didst receive it, why dost thou glory, as if thou hadst not received it?"*

When we fail to thank God, we fail to acknowledge the truth that every good and perfect gift comes from our Heavenly Father. Not walking in this truth leads us to become vain in our imaginations as we begin to think of ourselves more highly than we ought. We will talk more about thanksgiving as a powerful antidote to pride later, but it is absolutely vital that we humble ourselves through giving thanks and recognize the joyous truth that everything we have has indeed been given to us by our Heavenly Father.

Before you continue reading, I urge you to get on your knees before God. Enter the presence of God with thanksgiving. Ask for His forgiveness for your ungratefulness and complaining, and begin to give thanks to the Lord, not because you feel good or everything in your life is going well, but because He is good and His mercy endures forever.

CHAPTER THREE

PREMEDITATED THANKSGIVING

THE FOUNDATIONAL REASON that you and I must give thanks in all things is because God commands us to do so. Why should we do what God commands us to do? Because God is worthy of our obedience.

Another reason to give thanks in everything is because of the incredible reality that the God, Who commands us to give thanks, is in control and has a purpose for everything in our lives. God uses all things to accomplish His purpose in our lives, and we abound in opportunities to give thanks to Him Who is in control of everything.

It is important for us to understand God's reason for instructing us to give thanks in everything because *what we believe affects whether or not we give thanks.* If I give thanks because I believe it will make me happy, and my goal is to be happy, then I am resting on a shaky foundation. If I give thanks because God commands me to and because He says all things are working together for good, then I have reason to give thanks no matter what.

Understanding the foundational purpose for a command provides us with reasons to endure the hardship involved in obedience, because we start to see a bigger picture and how the command fits into it. In fact, failing to understand the foundational purpose of giving thanks in everything may lead to dangerous misconceptions. If we focus exclusively on the blessings that come from giving thanks (such as increased joy and contentment), this focus can be evidence that we are slipping into humanistic thinking.

What do I mean by humanistic? One way to think of humanism is as a philosophy where the goal of all things is personal happiness. This wrong concept is easy to accept and quickly creeps into our mindsets even as believers. Humanistic thinking says that the goal of all things, including giving thanks, is for the purpose of personal happiness.

How often do I do something good, hoping that, if I do it, *I* will be better, *I* will be happier, and things will go better for *me*? Now, all of that may very well be true! My life may be happier and things will go better for me if I do what God has told me to do. However, such self-centered mindsets are evidence of a dangerous belief: the false idea that the Christian life is about me. Truly, we should live for a greater and more controlling life purpose than personal happiness.

This contrast between godly and humanistic thinking closely relates to thanksgiving because it strikes at the root of our motivation for giving thanks. The reason we are to give thanks in everything is not so that we will be blessed, feel happy, and enjoy life more; we are to give thanks in everything because our Lord, who has commanded us to give thanks, is worthy of all praise! (See Revelation 7:12.) When our goal is God's glory and not our personal happiness, we begin to walk in agreement with God by giving thanks. This thanksgiving flows out of the abundance of a heart that truly understands and embraces God's purpose.

We give thanks to God because He is worthy. Whatever trial we are facing, whatever difficulty we are in the midst of, God calls us to give thanks. He is not calling us to give thanks because it will make us feel better, nor because it is easy, but because He is worthy. In essence, the reason I give thanks is not for me, but for the glory of the Lord. The end of thanksgiving, its purpose and goal, is for the Lord to be glorified. There is no doubt that we reap untold blessings as a result of giving thanks in everything, but those blessings are amazing byproducts, not the goal. When we understand that the end goal of giving thanks is God's glory, we have a solid purpose for giving thanks.

Now that we have concluded that the foundation for giving thanks in everything is the worthiness and pleasure of God, let us look at a few more core truths that are foundational for understanding why God commands us to give thanks in everything.

I have had various opportunities to share about thanksgiving with a number of different audiences. Many times, I will ask for a show of hands in answer to the question: "How many of you believe that God is sovereign?" Most people raise their hand. Most of us are quick to claim that we believe God is sovereign. If I believe that God is sovereign, then I know that everything that comes into my life is either caused by God or allowed by God to accomplish His eternal purpose. If that is so, then shouldn't we respond to everything with thanksgiving? How can I claim that I believe God is sovereign if I murmur and complain and act as if there are problems in my life that God has let slip through the cracks and failed to solve? God is not sovereign unless He is in control of everything. Since God is in control of everything, I am duty bound to give thanks to Him.

Our murmuring and complaining is evidence that we do not yet fully believe the truth that God is sovereign. Our concept of God affects whether or not we give thanks in all things. If we believe He is sovereign and that He is working all things together for good for His wonderful purpose, how can we not give thanks in everything? The more we believe the truth about Who God is, the clearer we understand why He commands us to give thanks in all things. God is always sovereign and He never ceases to be anything but good.

Joseph was a man who suffered some very intense trials and hardships. His own brothers sold him into slavery in Egypt. While there, Joseph was falsely accused by Potiphar's wife and thrown into a dungeon. According to our natural reasoning, we would tend to think that if anyone had a reason to become bitter, Joseph did. He was abandoned, falsely accused, and treated unjustly. However, instead of responding with anger and bitterness, Joseph saw that God, in His sovereignty, was working everything according to His purpose. When Joseph was finally reunited with his brothers, he forgave them and told them the secret of how he did not become bitter. It is a secret that reminds us of why we should give thanks even when we are facing loneliness, injustice, and betrayal. *"Now therefore be not grieved, nor angry with yourselves, that ye sold me hither: for God did send me before you to preserve life. For these two years hath the famine been in the land: and yet there are five years, in the which there shall neither be earing nor harvest"* (Genesis 45:5–6).

Later, we gain more insight into what Joseph believed about God's sovereignty. He told his brothers, *"But as for you,*

*ye thought evil against me; but God meant it unto good, to bring to
pass, as it is this day, to save much people alive. Now therefore fear
ye not: I will nourish you, and your little ones. And he comforted
them, and spake kindly unto them"* (Genesis 50:20–21).

Instead of focusing on his circumstances, Joseph focused
on the Lord and recognized that God had a purpose for allowing the trials. He realized that God, in His sovereignty, was
the One in charge of his life. As you and I receive a revelation
of the sovereignty of God, our lives cannot help but be radically changed. Instead of refusing to give thanks because our
personal happiness has not been fulfilled, we will wonder how
anyone could *not* give thanks! After all, if our sovereign God
watches over every detail of our lives and uses even difficulties
for His good purpose, how can we not give thanks?

Again, we see that what we believe about God affects
whether or not we give thanks. If, like Joseph, we believe that
God is sovereign, we will have reason to give thanks no matter
what happens to us. It is obvious, when we read the Bible, how
God used the tragedy of Joseph being sold into slavery for a
wonderful purpose. He was used to save the lives of many who,
it seems, would otherwise have starved because of the famine
in Egypt. The God of Joseph is our God, and although we
may not see what He is doing in our lives, we can trust that
He *is* working all things together for good if we love Him and
are called according to His purpose. The question is, will we
respond to that reality and give thanks in all things?

There is a profound difference between knowing truth
intellectually and believing truth in the heart. Intellectually,
I may know the fact that God is sovereign, but if I still murmur
and complain, my speech reveals that I do not fully believe

that God is sovereign and that He is good. Do you see the difference? If I both know and *believe* that God is sovereign, and also believe that God is good, then I will thank Him. Knowing about a truth intellectually may not change my behavior, but *believing* a truth will. My actions, and the words that come out of my mouth, reveal what I truly believe. I will not give thanks to God in sincerity unless I believe in my heart that He is sovereign and He is good.

The truth is the truth whether we believe it or not. When we believe the truth, our behavior radically changes. In Psalm 106:12 we read, *"Then believed they his words; they sang his praise."* When the children of Israel believed what the Lord had told them, praise came out of their mouth. It seems that the children of Israel had heard the truth and known about the truth, but it wasn't until they *believed* the truth that they sang praise.

When we face a very trying circumstance, or even a simple irritation, if we know and also believe that God is sovereign, we will give thanks. We may not see how God is working things out according to His eternal purpose or how God is bringing glory to Himself through the situation. Not knowing or seeing does not change the fact that we need to give thanks. We give thanks, not because we feel like it, but because God is worthy and He is sovereign. Thanksgiving and praise flow from a revelation of Who God is.

Another facet of God's character which compels us to give thanks is His goodness. *"O give thanks unto the LORD; for he is good; for his mercy endureth for ever"* (1 Chronicles 16:34). The goodness of God is an unchanging cause for thanksgiving. If things are going well for me, God is good, and if things are going terribly for me, God is still good. The goodness of God is unchanging, so I can give thanks to the Lord no matter what I am going through. Even if it feels like the entire world is falling down around me, God is still good and therefore I am still to give thanks.

If I merely know intellectually that God is good, I will probably not give thanks. On the other hand, if I truly believe that God is good and that His mercy endures forever, then even when I am going through difficult trials and struggles, I can still give thanks to the Lord. If we visited a doctor and he prescribed a bad-tasting medicine, our response to the medicine will be determined largely by what we believe about the doctor. If we believe that he is a good doctor, we will take the medicine, even though it tastes bad, because we trust the doctor. We trust that he has a purpose for the medicine he gave us. In the same way, when we believe that God is good, no matter how painful or difficult things may be in our lives, we have reason to give thanks, because we are trusting in God Who is sovereign and *good*.

I suspect that before reading this book, most of you knew that God is worthy of all praise, that He is sovereign, and that He is good. But do you believe these truths? If murmuring and complaining are constantly coming out of your mouth, that is evidence that you are not believing the truth about God. How do we move from merely knowing about the truth to actually *believing* the truth? The answer is simple but unfathomably important: we begin to believe the truth in our heart as we spend time thinking about the truth. As we think about, or meditate, on God's Word, the truth moves from our head to our heart. As we roll the Word of God over and over in our minds, we eventually, by the grace of God, come to believe the truth.

You and I must commit premeditated thanksgiving. What do I mean by "premeditated"? Premeditating something means you thought about it first. You may have heard the term "premeditated" in reference to a crime, such as if a person committed "premeditated murder." This simply means that the action was thought about before it was done.

Crimes are not the only things that are premeditated. Everything you and I do has been premeditated. There is never a time in your life that you have not thought about something before you did it. Our words and actions must pass through our minds before they will be performed in reality. Since we think about everything before we do it in life, it is crucial for us to be aware of what we are thinking, or meditating, on. The question is posed to each one of us: what are we meditating on? What we think about, what we meditate on, is who we become.

In Luke 6:45 we read, *"A good man out of the good treasure of his heart bringeth forth that which is good; and an evil man out of the evil treasure of his heart bringeth forth that which is evil: for of the abundance of the heart his mouth speaketh."*

The words that we speak are a fruit of what we have thought about. What you and I think about becomes what we believe, whether that belief be truth or lies. Even if we do not realize it, we all have an unseen system of belief. For example, you may have decided that the color blue is a nice color. I, on the other hand, may have thought about the color blue and come to the conclusion that it is a very ugly color. Now, we may never voice our opinions, but our differing thoughts about the color blue could be called our "belief system" about the color blue. When you see a blue car, your response might be, "That is a really nice car!" What you believe about the color blue results in a seemingly spontaneous expression of your pleasure in the blue car. I might see the same car and exclaim, "Now that is an ugly car!" I have thought about the color blue as unpleasant, and those thoughts are expressed out of my mouth. We may not realize it, but both of us have a belief system about a certain car that has been formed as a result of our thoughts about the color blue. Our words and reactions toward the blue car were a result of our belief system about the color blue.

Do you find yourself complaining and murmuring without even thinking about it? The truth is that you actually *have* thought about it, because out of the abundance of our belief systems, which are formed by what we think, our mouth speaks. Our behavior, such as complaining and grumbling, or perhaps giving thanks, is a byproduct, a fruit, of what we have been thinking about.

What we meditate on is what goes into our belief system and what goes into our belief system then plays out in our behavior. Understanding the vital role that our thought-life plays in giving thanks in everything affects how we approach the principle of giving thanks. It means that giving thanks in everything involves much more than trying to express a few grateful words whenever we can muster up the energy. Giving thanks in everything requires a much greater revolution. It means allowing God to take control of our minds and to cause us to meditate on the truth, on what He has said instead of how things look or how we may feel.

I did not *feel* good about getting my finger slammed in a tailgate or stepping in a nest of fire ants. In those situations, my natural response of complaining and grumbling was replaced with thanksgiving. Why? Because God was gaining control over my belief system as I meditated on His Word. As I received His thoughts, He was responding, through me, with gratefulness. He empowers us to give thanks in everything as we surrender our thoughts, and therefore our words and our actions, to Him.

If I realize that I have a problem with murmuring and complaining, my real problem is not with my mouth; the real issue is what I have treasured up in my heart, because out of the abundance of my heart, my mouth speaks. What am I treasuring up in my heart? Whatever my heart treasures I start believing, and it directs the course of my life. My heart condition determines whether I will live a life of gratefulness and thankfulness to God or a miserable life of grumbling and complaining. In order to give God thanks in everything we must realize that we need to be focusing on the goodness of God before we encounter situations where we are tempted to grumble. Otherwise, we will not be successful in our quest to give thanks in everything. In other words, when faced with a difficult situation or irritation, whatever is in our hearts is going to come out of our mouths, and we need to be ready.

If we try to give thanks whenever an irritating situation comes without having first meditated on the Word of God and on the character and nature of who God is, we will find that when the situation comes, whatever is in our heart will come out of our mouths. It will not be thanksgiving! But if we are treasuring up God's Word in our heart through meditating on it, when an irritating or difficult situation arrives, out of our mouths will naturally flow praise and thanksgiving.

Let me give you an illustration from my life. As I meditated on giving thanks in all things, my response to things I faced in life slowly began to change. I remember one time when I was in college and had just finished going through the dinner line. My plate was piled with delicious pasta and topped with creamy Alfredo sauce. I looked forward to enjoying one of my favorite dishes. I wanted something to drink before I sat down to eat. I grabbed a cup to fill with juice. But as I attempted to hold my plate in one hand and fill my cup with the other, the unthinkable happened. My Styrofoam plate piled with mouth-watering pasta and steaming sauce slipped from my fingers. My wonderful dinner landed face down on the carpeted floor!

My response to the situation surprised me. When the plate hit the floor, what popped out of my mouth almost instantly was "Praise the Lord!" Instead of grumbling or complaining, I was able to rejoice as I helped clean up the mess I made. My natural response to dropping a plate of one my favorite foods would not have been "Praise the Lord." I knew that the way I had responded was a supernatural work of God. When the plate dropped, I didn't have to stop and think, "Okay, this is an irritating situation. I want to get frustrated, but instead I will give thanks." Now, sometimes such an intentional choice to give thanks is exactly what is necessary. However, even then it is a result of previous meditation; I would not know that I was supposed to give thanks if I had not thought about God's command to give thanks in everything. A response of praise to God came out of my mouth without effort. Why? Because God led me to meditate on giving thanks long before I dropped the plate of pasta.

What we meditate on is crucial. If you surrender your mind to think on the Word of God day and night, He will be free to teach you and guide in His ways. Giving thanks comes as a fruit of meditating on God's Word.

God's Word describes to us Who He is: He is good, He is sovereign, and He is working together all things in our lives for His wonderful purpose. As we continue talking about thanksgiving, we should remember one thing: thinking on God's Word, hiding it in our hearts, is the only way to see giving thanks become our way of life. As we gaze at God's Word, as we treasure it and ponder it, His Spirit will be free to work in us the important command to give thanks.

Have you ever heard a message on the importance of one of God's commands, such as His command to give thanks in everything, and thought, "I am going to do that!" And then, almost right away, you found yourself complaining more frequently than ever before? The answer to this quandary is not to abandon the command, or even to try harder to fulfill it, but to allow God to take control of the very root of your belief system. Our belief system is a result of what we have thought about. Fulfilling God's commands, such as to give thanks, means meditating on the truth and letting it get down into your heart; then, by the power of Christ Who lives in you, it will play out in your actions. It is only as you and I meditate on the Word of God that thanksgiving and praise will come out of our mouths. Let us begin today to ponder and embrace the truth of God's sovereignty and goodness. Let us give God access to our innermost being, to our belief system. Giving thanks in everything begins this moment by meditating on God's Word. We must commit premeditated thanksgiving.

CHAPTER FOUR

ALWAYS AND
AT ALL TIMES

As I am on this journey of thanksgiving with the Lord, one thing He has deeply impressed upon me is that thanksgiving should be our full-time occupation—not only at some moments, but at all times. We should take God's command literally. It is not something we do only in the mornings, just before meals, or only when going through a trial. Even though these times are very important occasions to give thanks, we are commanded to always give thanks in all things.

As we have already noted, 1 Thessalonians 5:18 says, *"In everything give thanks; for this is the will of God in Christ Jesus concerning you."*

Let us take a look at the Greek word for "everything" used in this verse. It is a very important word that contains deep meaning. The Greek word is παντί and it means. . . *everything!* Often, we "translate" this verse in our minds and think, "In most things give thanks. . ." or "In those things which I can see how God is using for good, give thanks." However, this word "everything" means exactly what it says; we are to give thanks in everything.

Colossians 3:17 says, *"And whatsoever ye do in word or in deed, do all in the name of the Lord Jesus, giving thanks to God and the Father by him."* This verse expounds to us what the Lord means when He used the word "everything." *Everything* includes every deed we do and every word we speak. Words and actions are what our daily lives are made of, so this means that we should give thanks to the Lord all the time. How is this accomplished?

If our very lives are an expression of Christ because we are joined together in an intimate relationship with Him, this means that every word and deed is under God's control. What does God want us to do in everything? He wants us to give thanks. Giving thanks in everything is a way of life that flows from a relationship with Christ. It means that when we wake up in the morning, the first words out of our mouth should be "Thank You, Lord." It means that when we spend quiet time with the Lord, we should offer unto Him the sacrifice of thanksgiving. As we eat breakfast, our hearts should overflow with gratefulness for the provision of the Lord and we should give thanks unto Him. This way of life continues as we drive to work, take care of our children, work in the office, take a lunch break, and all throughout the day.

How is this continual thanksgiving possible? It is possible because we are one with God through Christ, and as we meditate on His Word day and night, words of thanksgiving and attitudes of gratefulness flow from us. Giving thanks means a conscious choice to surrender our thoughts, and our mouths, to the Lord every moment of the day.

As we go through life, there are so many exciting opportunities to give thanks to the Lord! Situations that we would naturally see as only trials or difficulties, God can help us to see as opportunities to give thanks. May the Lord open our eyes to see them for what they are: opportunities to give thanks to the Lord! If every trial, difficulty, and irritation is met with thanksgiving, then instead of dampening our gratefulness to God, those irritations become fuel that ignite even greater thanksgiving in our hearts. If we give thanks in everything as God has commanded us to, we find that everything that happens in our lives may be seen, and responded to, as opportunities instead of hindrances.

Living a life of giving thanks in *everything*, even things that are not easy, means that after an eventful day, as we go to sleep at night, we can look back with joy at how God's will has, in some measure, been fulfilled in our lives through our giving thanks that day. As we reminisce over the events of the day, we are in awe of the goodness He has shown us, and even our last words to Him at night are "Thank You, Lord!" We should not wait for feelings! Give thanks in obedience to the Lord.

The secret to giving thanks in all things is really not a secret at all; the secret is simply thanking God in all things! It means not waiting until things appear to be going better for us, or until we understand what God's plan for our lives is, but simply giving thanks right now. Giving thanks in everything is a way of life that flows from a bold faith in God, Who commands us to give thanks in everything, no matter what. We are told in Philippians 4:4, *"Rejoice in the Lord always and again I say rejoice."*

Has there ever been a time in your life when you could not seem to think of anything to thank God for? Here is something that has helped me to give thanks in times such as those.

Next time you cannot think of anything to give thanks for, stop and take a deep breath. There. You now have something to be thankful for: you were able to take a breath! Scripture says, *"Let every thing that hath breath praise the LORD. Praise ye the LORD"* (Psalm 150:6). Every breath we take is evidence of the kindness of God, Who gives us breath moment by moment. Even having the privilege of taking a breath is something for which we should give thanks. As long as we have breath to do so, we should be praising our Lord Who is worthy.

There is a difference also between thanksgiving and praise. The two are so closely connected that it is very difficult to differentiate between them. I believe that they often accompany one another. Hebrews 13:15 reads, *"By him therefore let us offer the sacrifice of praise to God continually, that is, the fruit of our lips giving thanks to his name."* One might say that praise is an all-encompassing word that describes magnifying and exalting God and Who He is, while giving thanks means specifically magnifying His goodness and exalting God for all He has done for us. Since all the Lord does is an expression of Who He is, giving thanks is intertwined with praising God. Both thanksgiving and praise turn our focus upon God instead of self.

As I have looked through Scripture, I have been staggered by the number of times that thanksgiving and praise are described as being something that we should do all the time. Following is a sample of some of the verses on the subject (emphasis added); take special note of words like *continually*, *forever*, and *always*.

I will bless the LORD at all times: **his praise shall continually be in my mouth.** (Psalm 34:1)

And my tongue shall speak of thy righteousness and of thy **praise all the day long.** (Psalm 35:28)

In God we boast **all the day long**, and **praise thy name for ever.** Selah. (Psalm 44:8)

I will make thy name to be remembered in all generations: therefore shall the people **praise thee for ever and ever.** (Psalm 45:17)

I will **praise thee for ever**, because thou hast done it: and I will wait on thy name; for it is good before thy saints. (Psalm 52:9)

So we thy people and sheep of thy pasture will **give thee thanks for ever**: we will shew forth thy praise to all generations. (Psalm 79:13)

Giving thanks always for all things unto God and the Father in the name of our Lord Jesus Christ. (Ephesians 5:20)

Rejoice in the Lord alway: and again I say, **Rejoice.** (Philippians 4:4)

And **whatsoever ye do in word or deed, do all** in the name of the Lord Jesus, **giving thanks to God** and the Father by him. (Colossians 3:17)

For this cause also **thank we God without ceasing,** because, when ye received the word of God which ye heard of us, ye received it not as the word of men, but as it is in truth, the word of God, which effectually worketh also in you that believe. (1 Thessalonians 2:13)

Rejoice evermore. (1 Thessalonians 5:16)

We are bound to thank God always for you, brethren, as it is meet, because that your faith groweth exceedingly, and the charity of every one of you all toward each other aboundeth. (2 Thessalonians 1:3)

By him therefore let us offer the **sacrifice of praise to God continually,** that is, the fruit of our lips giving thanks to his name. (Hebrews 13:15)

Each time I read through a list of verses such as these, it seems as if my mind has undergone a little more renovation as I see more clearly the importance of giving thanks all the time. Nearly half of the verses above are from the Psalms, which are full of rich and powerful praises to the Lord. If we want to learn more of what it looks like to thank the Lord in everything and to praise Him forever, we would do well to spend time reading and meditating on the book of Psalms.

When my family and I first moved to the south, we learned to anticipate one of the questions that people would ask. Often, people would say, "You are not from around here.

Where are you from?" They recognized that we were not originally from the south because we did not have a southern accent. Our northern accent revealed that we were from the north. The way we spoke was outward evidence of our identity as northerners. In the same way, you and I, as believers, should have an unmistakable accent of thanksgiving. Instead of the normal complaining and grumbling that the world has become so accustomed to, our tone of life should be that of rejoicing and thanksgiving. After all, giving thanks is God's will for our lives! We should be known, not as the irritated, complaining after-church crowd, but as those who are full of thanksgiving and praise.

Our lives should have such a mark of gratefulness on them that when you and I encounter others, they should be able to recognize that we "are not from around here," because our real citizenship is in heaven! (See Philippians 3:20.) If I came and told you, with a thick southern drawl, that I am from the north, you would have a hard time believing me! In the same way, if we as believers say that we serve a God who is sovereign and good and that we are walking in His will, but our "accent" is one of murmuring and complaining, the world will have a hard time believing us!

My family and I did not try to sound like we were from the north; our northern accent was the manner in which we naturally spoke. It came to us naturally regardless of who we were talking with or what was going on around us. An accent is not a one-time event; it is the spontaneous expression of who we are. Thanksgiving is the same. Giving thanks is a result of a heart surrendered to God, and that means we should be giving thanks always and at all times. Giving thanks is not a one-time event—it is the accent of a Christian. As we meditate on God's Word, and especially on His command to give thanks, and as we do all things within the name of Christ, our accent becomes the accent of thanksgiving and that accent naturally reveals itself always and at all times.

When a composer writes music, they usually write it in a major or minor key, which goes a long way in choosing the "mood" of the song. If a song originally written in a major key is transposed to a minor key, the whole sense of the song changes. The "key" of the Christian life, of a life hidden with Christ in God and orchestrated by a good and sovereign God Who is working all things together for good, should be the key of thanksgiving. If you and I try to live the Christian life in the key of murmuring and complaining, our lives take on a discordant note. It is important to remember that even if an entire song is played in the correct key, but one or two of the notes of the song are played in a different key, the entire song is affected. It is easy for us to understand that for a song to be played correctly, the entire song must be in agreement. In the same way, it is vitally important that we give thanks in *everything*. Every area of our life, every irritation, trial, or joy, is part of the bigger picture of the will of God. If even one "note" is off key, the entire song will be affected. Let us, through the power of Christ Who lives in us, begin to give thanks at all times and in everything.

CHAPTER FIVE

RETURNING AND RELATIONSHIP

LUKE 17 GIVES a powerful account about giving thanks. We read the incredible story of Jesus healing ten lepers. As Jesus traveled through Samaria and Galilee, He was met by ten men. They were not average men; they were stricken with the horrific disease of leprosy. *"And as he entered into a certain village, there met him ten men that were lepers, which stood afar off: And they lifted up their voices, and said, Jesus, Master, have mercy on us"* (Luke 17:12–13).

Their voices were probably filled with desperation: "Jesus, Master, have mercy on us!" They cried out to Jesus, but it sounds as if their faith was limited. These men wanted Jesus to heal them—they were asking Him to do that—but they did not draw near to Him. I wonder if these men were half-hoping that Jesus would heal them, but still doubtful and hanging back in fear and uncertainty. Jesus saw them and addressed their need by instructing them to go and show themselves to the priests. This was what the law required them to do if they thought they no longer had leprosy. Obediently, the lepers headed to go see the priest. As they went, they were healed. This is an astounding miracle!

At that time, leprosy was considered an incurable disease. One way leprosy affects the body is by causing a lack of feeling in nerve endings, which keeps the sick person from feeling pain. So, someone with leprosy might hurt themselves badly, have an infection, or suffer any host of other problems and not even realize it. This can result in horrors such as the loss of limbs and appendages. We can only speculate what kinds of deformities and physical defects these men may have been afflicted with. As they went to fulfill Jesus' command, they experienced the miracle of His healing of them. This horrible disease that had wrecked their lives was gone! Their skin was clear and their nerve endings must have had their sensitivity restored.

Imagine the delight these ten men felt as they realized what Jesus did for them. It was as if He gave them their lives back! In those days, leprosy was a disease that prevented the sufferers from being near their families, working with other people, and simply carrying on daily life. Instead, those stricken with leprosy lived separate from society as beggars under constant suspicion, shame, and sickness. Suddenly, these ten men could hug their children. They could actually earn a living, carry on conversations with the public, be with those they loved, walk into town, go to feasts, and be respectable members of a community! It was as if, by healing their leprosy, Jesus threw open the doorway of their lives, and now opportunities came rushing at them like a tidal wave.

With so many new possibilities for life glowing before them, perhaps we can understand why nine of the lepers failed to return to thank Jesus. They were too busy. Now they had so many opportunities that they could have only dreamed of before. Their new sense of freedom, which Jesus gave by healing them, captured their full attention. They forgot to take care of the most important business first: to give glory to God.

Not all of the lepers were distracted from giving God glory. One of them, a Samaritan, kept his focus on Jesus. As soon as he was healed, he did something that the others did not take time to do: he gave glory to God with a loud voice. When God works in our lives, we should respond the same way this leper responded. He stopped, turned away from everything else, and thanked God. *"And one of them, when he saw that he was healed, turned back, and with a loud voice glorified God"* (Luke 17:15).

The Lord has done so many incredible miracles in our lives. Jesus washed us from our sins, gave us eternal life, provides for our needs, causes the sun to rise every morning, gives us breath, keeps our heart beating, and pours His blessing upon us in countless ways. Have we acknowledged this? Have we ever turned back from the tidal wave of life, fallen on our faces before our Savior, and thanked Him *personally* for His great work, as the Samaritan leper did? Or do we respond as the other nine lepers? It was not enough for the nine other lepers to feel grateful for Jesus' work in their lives. They needed to stop, return, and verbally give glory to God. Everything God does in our lives is good, because He is good. (See Psalm 119:68.) This means that we have a reason to give thanks in everything. It is not enough for us to feel grateful; we must express it with our mouths and give glory to God.

Continuing the narrative in Luke 17, we see that only one former leper, the Samaritan, gave glory to God. He experienced something that the other nine lepers missed. The other lepers got to see Jesus, got to hear Jesus, and were powerfully healed by Jesus. Yet they stood afar off. They did not draw near to Him like the Samaritan. This one leper returned and *"fell down on his face at his feet, giving him thanks: and he was a Samaritan"* (Luke 17:16).

Thanksgiving is a special way we can draw close to the Lord; this underscores why we should personally give thanks to the Lord. God desires that we would draw near to Him, and thanksgiving is an intimate way to do that.

God created us for closeness to Him. Giving thanks is not an item on a checklist or a self-help tip. When we turn aside from the busy things of life to give thanks to the Lord like this leper did, a door opens up for greater intimacy with God.

Let's listen to how Jesus responded to the Samaritan's thanksgiving: *"And Jesus answering said, Were there not ten cleansed? but where are the nine? There are not found that returned to give glory to God, save this stranger. And he said unto him, Arise, go thy way: thy faith hath made thee whole"* (Luke 17:17–19).

Why did Jesus say, "thy faith hath made thee whole" instead of "your faith has healed you?" I wonder, since leprosy victims sometimes suffer from deformities, if maybe this was so with the ten lepers who came to Jesus. Perhaps they had lost some of their appendages or limbs. Could it be that when Jesus told the leper that gave Him thanks, "your faith has made you *whole,*" that this Samaritan had his appendages, and perhaps even limbs, restored? Could it be that the other nine lepers walked away with the incredible gift of being healed, but only the Samaritan walked away both healed and made whole?

This story clearly illustrates the power of thanksgiving. The command to give thanks in everything is part of God's desire for a close relationship with us. Our natural tendency is to turn even glorious principles from God's Word such as giving thanks in everything into lifeless formulas. Let me reiterate: giving thanks is not about marking something off a checklist; it is about returning to give glory to God and therefore walking in a new depth of relationship with Him. Every irritation is an invitation to enter into the presence of God as we receive it with thanksgiving. One of God's purposes is fellowship. Complaining and murmuring hinder us from communion with the Lord. A lack of thankfulness is an impediment to a living, personal relationship with Jesus. Giving thanks is glorious because, as we return to give glory to God, we find that He is there ready to receive our thanks, to reveal Himself to us, and to make us whole as never before!

Giving thanks is about having communion and fellowship with the Lord in everything. God has called each one of us to be like this Samaritan, to turn aside and fall on our faces and give thanks to the Lord for the great things He has done. As we turn again and again in thanksgiving, we will find an intimacy with Him that is astonishing.

A wonderful aspect of walking in an abiding relationship with the Lord involves being in His presence. Psalms 95:2 says, *"Let us come before his presence with thanksgiving, and make a joyful noise unto him with psalms."*

We hear so much about the presence of God, but how do we come before His presence? We know that God is omnipresent, so, if God is everywhere, are we not always in His presence? In many ways, yes, we are. God is omnipresent, so His presence is with us wherever we go. (See Psalm 139:7–10.) However, there is a vast difference from *being* somewhere, such as in the presence of our omnipresent God, and *having fellowship* with someone. The difference between being in God's presence and entering God's presence is not hard to understand if we look through the lens of our everyday relationships with people. Picture a man boarding a packed subway in New York City. Upon entering, he squeezes in amongst the crowd of men and women. The crowd is very close; they are literally standing shoulder to shoulder. The individuals on the subway are in the presence of the man, but they do not look him in the eye. They are staring into the distance or glancing at their phones. None of them had fellowship with him. Then the man got off the subway and arrived home. His wife and children crowd around him eagerly asking questions and sharing news with him. Once again, the man is in the presence of people, but instead of merely being in their presence, he has rich fellowship with them. What changed? The people in both scenarios were in the presence of the man, but one group had no fellowship with him because they did not recognize him or talk with him. On the other hand, the man's family was in his presence *and* had rich fellowship with him because they recognized him, loved him, and communed with him. The second group was not merely *in* the man's presence, they *entertained* his presence.

I believe that when we give thanks, we are entertaining the presence of God. The psalmist tells us *"...thou art holy, O thou that inhabitest the praises of Israel"* (Psalm 22:3).

The Lord inhabits the praises of His people as a place of settled residence. Do we want the Lord to dwell and reside with us? Part of entertaining His presence, of knowing His abiding with us and in us, is praising the Lord. Is that not what giving thanks is all about? When we give thanks, we give glory to God. When we glorify God, falling down at His feet with praise, adoration, and thankfulness like the Samaritan leper did, we experience His presence in a new way.

The omnipresence of God means that there is nowhere we can go where God is not present. Praising God is entertaining and celebrating His presence in a special way. When we praise God, we enjoy His presence that is always available to us. 2 Chronicles 5 describes how the children of Israel finished building the temple of the Lord and then gathered together to dedicate the temple. They brought in the holy vessels and the ark of the covenant. Yet, despite their actions, the cloud, which I believe represented the tangible evidence of God's presence, did not fill the temple. They offered many sacrifices to the Lord, which was necessary preparation, yet the cloud still did not fill the temple. It was not until the Levites began thanking and praising the Lord that the cloud filled the temple.

> Also the Levites which were the singers, all of them of Asaph, of Heman, of Jeduthun, with their sons and their brethren, being arrayed in white linen, having cymbals and psalteries and harps, stood at the east end of the altar, and with them an hundred and twenty priests sounding with trumpets:) It came even to pass, as the trumpeters and singers were as one, to make one sound to be heard in praising and thanking the LORD; and when they lifted up their voice with the trumpets and cymbals and instruments of musick, and praised the LORD, saying, For he is good; for his mercy endureth for ever: that then the house was filled with a cloud, even the house of the LORD. (2 Chronicles 5:12–13)

The cloud did not fill the temple until the people began thanking and praising the Lord. You and I are like the temple. 1 Corinthians 6:19 says, *"What? know ye not that your body is the temple of the Holy Ghost which is in you, which ye have of God, and ye are not your own?"*

The cloud, the physical manifestation of His presence, only descended on the temple when the people of Israel began praising and thanking the Lord; you and I only entertain the Lord's presence when we give thanks to Him. The Lord inhabits the praises of His people. His presence is always with us, but when we give thanks to God, we become aware of His presence in a special way and experience more fully what it means to abide in His presence.

After Jesus arose from the dead, before He ascended into heaven, He told His disciples, *"And, behold, I send the promise of my Father upon you: but tarry ye in the city of Jerusalem, until ye be endued with power from on high"* (Luke 24:49). What did this tarrying mean for the disciples? Later in this same chapter, we read that they *"...were continually in the temple, praising and blessing God. Amen"* (Luke 24:53).

While the disciples were waiting for the promise of the Holy Spirit to be poured out upon them, they were constantly praising and blessing the Lord. We know that the Lord fulfilled His promise and poured the Holy Spirit out upon His people, and it is no coincidence that they were living a grateful life. Thanking and praising the Lord opens the way for us to entertain the presence of God as never before. By commanding us to give thanks in everything, God guides us in walking in relationship with Him, entertaining His presence, and being filled with His Spirit. Giving thanks in everything is about a relationship with the living God.

It is important to remember that giving thanks in everything, and therefore entertaining the Lord's presence in everything, is not an emotionally-defined experience. In other words, the power of giving thanks in everything should not be measured by whether or not we *feel* God's presence. The work of God in our hearts and lives goes far deeper than our emotions. The children of Israel were not looking for feelings when they praised God. They were seeking to walk in obedience to God and to entertain His presence. The disciples were not searching after emotions as they praised and blessed the Lord continually in the temple. In the same way, you and I may not feel God's presence as we thank and praise Him, but we can be assured that His presence is with us.

The purpose of our thanksgiving is not for our own benefit or feelings; our thanksgiving is for the pleasure of God. God is worthy of our lives, so we should give Him what He is seeking: thanks and praise. God guarantees His presence with us, but He does not always guarantee anything regarding our feelings. It is important to remember that to give thanks in everything is our duty and is a part of entering God's presence whether or not we feel it. Giving thanks in everything is a demonstration that we believe His Word, the only solid foundation, and are not living our lives centered on the shifting sands of emotions.

Beware of living like the nine lepers who rushed into their daily lives, enjoying God's gift but missing out on a relationship with the Giver. Instead, let us return and give glory to God with a loud voice. As we recognize His presence, we will come to experience communion with Him that we have never known before. Let us, through the power of Christ, give thanks in everything and experience what it is to be made whole by Him.

CHAPTER SIX

THANKSGIVING, THE ANTIDOTE

WHY DO WE, even after hearing the truth about thanksgiving, continue complaining and grumbling? The secret poison that causes us to complain also hinders us from the glorious privilege and high calling of knowing God personally. This poison, which is a deadly hindrance to our walk with the Lord and a root cause of ungratefulness, is the poison of pride. A lack of thankfulness demonstrates a heart that believes it deserves what it gets, instead of recognizing its unworthiness and God's unmerited generosity. Humility is like the antidote that gives us deliverance from pride. Humility and thanksgiving go hand in hand.

It is easy to understand the relationship between humility and thanksgiving. If you saw someone give a beggar a one-hundred-dollar bill, and the beggar took the money, stuck it in their pocket, and walked away without saying a word of thanks, what would you think? You would probably marvel that the beggar did not value the gift enough to say thank you for it! Suppose you then questioned the beggar about their lack of gratefulness and they replied, "I do not have to say thank you.

I earned the hundred dollars." What would you think? Their words would indicate that they were refusing to acknowledge that they had been given a gift they did not deserve. They would see no need to give thanks if they thought they provided the gift for themselves.

It is plain that the beggar's ungratefulness stemmed from pride. Similarly, when we fail to give thanks in everything, we are not humbling ourselves under the truth of our need and God's generosity. If the beggar said, "Thank you so much! I really needed the money!" it would be a humbling position for him as he recognized the generosity of the giver. It is the same with us. Everything we have has been given to us by God. Often, we prefer to believe that we deserve something or earned it ourselves when actually we depend on God for everything. We need to humble ourselves, recognize our absolute dependence, and give thanks. How can we not express gratefulness to God once we understand, like the Samaritan leper understood, that God has given us what we could not provide for ourselves, and that He is worthy of being thanked and praised?

Our response to gifts that are given to us is to say thank you. If we were given a gift, but thought that we earned it, we probably would not thank the giver because we would not think it was a gift. Our response to the gift, in that case, would be prideful. As you and I turn from pride and humble ourselves before God, He brings us deeper in our relationship with Him. Pride keeps us from depending on God and realizing His presence, whereas thanking God is part of coming to Him and experiencing more of what it means to abide in His care. *"Every good gift and every perfect gift is from above, and cometh down from the Father of lights, with whom is no variableness, neither shadow of turning"* (James 1:17).

When we face trials and hardship, we must humble ourselves and give thanks to the Lord, knowing that the Lord works all things together for good to those who love Him and are called according to His purpose. Yet, while trials and suffering often cause us to turn to God in desperation and reveal our need for Him, there is an equally important occasion in which we should recognize God and give thanks: when everything is going great. The nine lepers demonstrated the danger of not doing this when they neglected to thank God when things were going well for them.

Have you ever gone through a trying time in your life and been brought to a place of humility before the Lord? Perhaps you sought His will for your life and discovered His command to rejoice and give thanks in the midst of difficulty. So you gave thanks, trusted in God, and experienced His blessing, presence, and deliverance. But what happened after a little time passed? Most of us quickly forget what the Lord has done for us when things are going well. We are quick to listen to the poisonous voice of pride that tells us we earned our achievements by ourselves. This is part of the reason that it is important to give thanks in everything. Everything includes both prosperous and joyous times as well as difficult ones. The danger of forgetting about God when times are easy can be seen over and over in the saga of God's relationship with the children of Israel. The children of Israel turned to God in times of distress and danger but were quick to forget about Him. Their lack of thankfulness and praise was not because they were suffering in some great way, but because they were prospering! The Lord warned the children of Israel:

> When thou hast eaten and art full, then thou shalt
> bless the Lord thy God for the good land which
> he hath given thee. Beware that thou forget not
> the Lord thy God, in not keeping his command-
> ments, and his judgments, and his statutes, which I
> command thee this day: Lest when thou hast eaten
> and art full, and hast built goodly houses, and dwelt
> therein; And when thy herds and thy flocks multi-
> ply, and thy silver and thy gold is multiplied, and
> all that thou hast is multiplied; Then thine heart be
> lifted up, and thou forget the Lord thy God, which
> brought thee forth out of the land of Egypt, from
> the house of bondage. (Deuteronomy 8:12–14)

What is the root of the lie that would cause us to forget
the Lord, just as the children of Israel did? What meditation
results in such pride? As we read further, we discover the kinds
of thoughts that will keep us from returning to give glory to
God like the Samaritan leper:

> And thou say in thine heart, My power and the
> might of mine hand hath gotten me this wealth.
> But thou shalt remember the Lord thy God: for it
> is he that giveth thee power to get wealth, that he
> may establish his covenant which he sware unto thy
> fathers, as it is this day. (Deuteronomy 8:17–18)

Just as He blessed and cared for His people Israel, the Lord
has blessed you and me in incredible ways. Have we returned
to give glory to Him and thank Him, or have we tasted the
poison of pride and continued on in life without recognizing

our Heavenly Father? How do we keep from forgetting the marvelous things the Lord has done? By partaking of what could be called the "antidote" for pride: giving thanks in everything! As we learned earlier, giving thanks begins with meditating on God's Word. As we meditate upon His Word and therefore give thanks out of a heart of gratefulness, we live in the reality of our dependence upon God instead of giving in to pride. When we give thanks to the Lord, we are calling to mind His goodness and mercy to us. By the grace of God, let us repent of our ungratefulness. Let us humble ourselves before God and choose to say "thank you" to Him for Who He is and all He has done. After all, He is worthy of all praise, honor, thanks, and glory!

Nebuchadnezzar is another example of one who believed the lie that he earned his accomplishments without God's help. A powerful and wealthy king, Nebuchadnezzar was poisoned with pride after he experienced success in his kingdom. He spoke out of the abundance of his heart that had not been humbled before God through giving thanks. We read in Daniel 4:30 what Nebuchadnezzar said: *"The king spake, and said, Is not this great Babylon, that **I** have built for the house of the kingdom by the might of **my** power, and for the honour of **my** majesty?"* (emphasis added).

Nebuchadnezzar did not give thanks because he did not recognize that everything he had was given to him. What was the result of this pride, this lack of thankfulness to God, that Nebuchadnezzar walked in? God brought him down to a deeply humiliating place of becoming like an animal and eating grass like an ox until he learned and received the truth. When God had finally brought him to a place of humility, Nebuchadnezzar declared, *"Now I Nebuchadnezzar praise and extol and honour the*

King of heaven, all whose works are truth, and his ways judgment:
and those that walk in pride he is able to abase" (Daniel 4:37).
When we give thanks to the Lord, we are focusing on the
Lord instead of on ourselves. Like Nebuchadnezzar, when we
learn to praise, extol, and honor the King of heaven, we have
no time to complain and murmur. Everything that we have is
what we have been given. As we meditate on that reality, we are
humbled before the Lord and the result is a heart of thankfulness. All of this demonstrates that it is vitally important for us
to understand two things. First, we have to see that all we have
is what we have been given; there is nothing we can take credit
for or demand from God. Secondly, our occupation must not
be thinking about ourselves and what we have accomplished
and attained, but rather with praising the Lord.

Sometimes God will allow challenges in our lives to
humble us. They can range in size from small irritations to
major trials. In my life, God has used difficulties I have faced
to humble me and challenge me to give thanks to Him. Two
unexpected situations stand out. I was helping as a backup
photographer for a camp, and I really wanted to get some
good pictures. One evening, they had a rodeo-type event with
a Christian speaker who uses horse training as an object lesson
to talk about the Christian life. The audience was going to be
seated outdoors in bleachers around the corral, with large lights
on the tall poles shining down, and the speaker was going to
be sharing in the center with his horses. It was a great moment
to capture through a picture! At the same event, a friend of
mine was doing small airplane rides for the camp attendees. I
thought a photograph from above the corral would be ideal,
so I asked my friend if he would be willing to fly me up above
everything going on for a photo shoot.

Just before the rodeo event was going to start, I climbed into the cockpit of the small airplane next to my pilot friend, with my camera in hand. We taxied down the runway and took off into the beautiful early evening sky. We flew above cow pastures, ponds, and bluffs as we made a big loop to head over to the coral. The rugged Texas landscape was so scenic; I wanted to get a picture with my new smartphone. I recently purchased this smartphone because of its high-quality camera and I was excited to use it. I pulled it out of my pocket, but I found it difficult to get a good shot through the glare of the airplane window. The pilot told me something I did not know: I could open the window! I had only flown commercially before this time, so opening the window while flying was a new concept to me.

I popped the window open and once again began to try to get a photo of the scenery. As I focused on taking pictures, I did not realize how much wind was coming across the front of the plane and whipping past the window. All of the sudden, much to my dismay, the wind caught my phone and ripped it right out the window! I could not believe that I had just dropped my phone out of an airplane window. I was distressed at what had just happened, and I began to feel frustration welling up inside of me. How could I have possibly allowed that expensive new smartphone to slip out of my fingers and fall out the window?! My pride began to kick in as I thought how humiliating it would be to tell people that I had dropped it out of an airplane. As the frustration and pride bubbled up in me, God prompted me to give thanks in everything.

Honestly, it was hard to give thanks right then. I certainly did not feel like thanking the Lord at that moment. The Lord faithfully reminded me that I had preached about giving thanks; now it was time to live it. At first, my thanksgiving was a little feeble, but as I started to praise and thank the Lord, I began to sense the Lord's peace. I was still bothered about losing my phone, but there was an awareness of the Lord's peace in the midst of it as I took this invitation to enter His presence with thanksgiving.

After I took the picture of the rodeo event with my other camera (with the strap securely around my neck to keep it from falling!), we flew back to the runway. As the plane landed, I prayed a simple prayer asking the Lord to show us where the dropped phone was. We knew it was somewhere in a roughly one-hundred-acre radius. This area included cow pastures, trees, ponds, and bluffs. Since it was evening, the sun had just set, and the chances of actually finding the phone seemed very slim. Even if we did succeed and find it, it seemed impossible that the phone would not be broken after being dropped from such a height.

We drove out to the general area where we thought the phone could be; it was like looking for a needle in a haystack. We did not know where to start. Discouraged, we climbed into the car and started driving back. Someone in the car suggested that perhaps we could use technology to find the phone. My smartphone had a GPS technology built into it to help locate it if lost, but even if my phone had survived the fall (which seemed unlikely), I did not know if I had the GPS enabled. I figured it was worth a try. I logged into my phone's account from a laptop and activated the search feature. The computer showed a compass on the screen as it calculated where the phone was. We watched with rapt attention as a map appeared on the computer screen, showing us the cow pasture on campus, and there, not far from a scrubby tree, was a glowing dot in the pasture. It was my phone!

We hurried outside, jumped in the car, drove down the road, climbed over a barbed wire fence into the cow pasture, and there, lying in the grass, was my smartphone! I picked the phone up and to my amazement, there was not a scratch on it that I could see, and it still worked great. I was thrilled. It was easy to give thanks now! My heart overflowed with gratefulness to the Lord for this wonderful little blessing, allowing us to find the phone, and incredibly, it was undamaged.

I believe that sometimes God waits to work in a given situation until we begin to give Him thanks and praise. God lives in the praises of His people. (See Psalm 22:3.) When we give thanks, we invite Him into every situation in our lives, and He works in powerful ways as a result.

Maybe you are thinking that it is wonderful that my story with dropping my phone worked out so well; maybe you are mulling over the fact that your situation did not work out like that. Maybe you have faced much greater challenges that did not have happy endings. Actually, this story was not over, and God was not done teaching me.

A few months after the airplane incident, I was out fishing on a lake in a canoe. I turned in the canoe to get a lure, and when I did, the whole canoe rocked sideways. I almost fell into the water; gratefully, I kept the canoe from tipping over. I was feeling relieved that I did not fall into the water when I realized, much to my chagrin, that when I rocked sideways, my smartphone slipped out of my pocket into the cold lake water. I could not believe it. The very same phone that survived a drop from an airplane was now at the bottom of the lake! The Lord reminded me to give thanks even in the midst of this. In obedience to His prompting, I began to thank Him for this second loss of my phone.

A couple of guys with some diving experience were willing to swim to the bottom of the lake to try to locate the phone. As they searched, I was hopeful that they would find the phone and that it would still work. I thought about what an amazing story it would be to be able to share with people that the very same phone that made it through the skydiving experience unscathed also survived a dip in the lake. The guys tried their best to find it, but the phone must have gotten down into the weeds at the bottom of the lake, because they were unable to locate it. I was sad that my phone was lost and unable to be found. Why, the first time I thanked God for dropping my phone, did the story end how I wanted, and the second time did it not end the way I would have chosen?

God used these two experiences to teach me an important lesson. When we give thanks to the Lord in the trials we face, God works. Sometimes He works by entering into the situation and radically changing it, like in the first story of dropping my phone and then recovering it undamaged. Yet sometimes, perhaps more often than not, when we express our thankfulness to God, our challenging situations stay the same, but God uses them to change us and conform us more to the image of His Son. Sometimes, God will both change the outward circumstances *and* use the trials in our lives to change us. However God chooses to work, we can trust Him in it and express our trust through thanking Him. May the Lord give us the grace to give thanks in everything and see Him work powerfully in our lives in whatever way He sees fit. May this thanksgiving flow out of a trust that the Lord knows what He is doing and that He does all things well.

CHAPTER SEVEN

PRAYING WITH THANKSGIVING

MY JOURNEY OF learning to give thanks has been both challenging and exciting and has influenced so many areas in my life. This includes the way that I think, the words I speak, and how I live. God has used giving thanks to do many things in me, but one of the areas in which thanksgiving has affected me has been in my prayer life. We saw in an earlier chapter that God inhabits the praises of His people, so when our prayer closet is full of thanksgiving to the Lord, we find our time with Him is enriched and that our prayers are infused afresh with His power.

Giving thanks in everything is one of the secrets to powerful prayer—although it can hardly be called a secret, because over and over in His Word, God tells us in very clear terms that we *must* give thanks to Him when we pray. Philippians 4:6 says, *"Be careful for nothing but in everything by prayer and supplication with thanksgiving let your requests be made known unto God."*

The word translated "careful" in this verse means to be anxious. I am sorry to say that you and I often come to prayer as those who are distracted and anxious for many things instead of careful for nothing! This is not how God has told us to pray, but what else are we to do when we pray if we do not worry out loud as we are used to doing? How should we pray without anxiety? God has given us the answer. The answer is in every-thing, by prayer and supplication, with thanksgiving, make our requests known to Him. This manner of prayer is not an option or a helpful suggestion but a command. When God commands us to pray without ceasing and to give thanks in everything, it is not hard to see that prayer and thanksgiving are inseparably intertwined.

Imagine that you need something and want to go ask someone you trust for their assistance. The first step to approach them is to enter their presence. It is logical to think about entering someone's presence in order to speak to them. What is one aspect of entering God's presence? We enter His gates with thanksgiving and His courts with praise.

Psalm 100:4 says, *"Enter into his gates with thanksgiving, and into his courts with praise: be thankful unto him, and bless his name."* It is a spiritual work that cannot be fully explained, but when we give thanks to God, we entertain His presence in a special way. When we begin our times of prayer with giving thanks, we find that our focus is not on the problems, puzzles, or even the people we are praying for. Instead, we are magnifying the Lord and looking to Him. When we look to Him, we become more aware of the truth of His presence. 1 Timothy 2:1 informs us that an aspect of praying for others is giving thanks for them: *"I exhort therefore, that, first of all, supplications, prayers, intercessions, and giving of thanks, be made for all men[.]"*

As believers in the Lord Jesus Christ, we are not in a war against flesh and blood, but against principalities, powers, and rulers of darkness and spiritual wickedness in high places. (See Ephesians 6:12.) Prayer is not a ritual that consists of listing our worries and wants to God. Instead, it is entering the front lines of a spiritual battle. 1 Timothy 2 is not a nice idea that might be good for us to follow. It is a battle plan from our Captain. When we come before God in prayer, seeking victory in the spiritual realm, we need to be following His battle plans.

How has He instructed us to come before Him in prayer? He has commanded us to not only make supplications and prayers and intercessions, but also, specifically, to give thanks. If we meditate on thanksgiving in light of spiritual warfare, it makes perfect sense that God commands us to give thanks when we pray, because that is glorying in the victory that He has already won! Giving thanks is part of recognizing our victory in Christ. When we give thanks, we proclaim to the spiritual forces that God is Ruler and Victor. There is much more that can be said about giving thanks and spiritual victory and we will discuss it more in a later chapter, but right now it suffices to say that prayer, when combined with praise and when filled with thanksgiving to God, is a powerful weapon that God uses to reveal His victory over the world, the flesh, and the devil.

Paul exhorted Timothy that along with supplications, prayers, and intercessions, thanksgiving should be made for all men. How easy it is, when beginning in prayer for someone, to begin with words such as, "Lord, please bring so-and-so to salvation. Please speak to their hearts and heal their sickness." God greatly desires that we make requests for others and intercede for them, but we see in Scripture that God wants us to go further. When praying for those he cared for, Paul consistently gave thanks for them. *"Wherefore I also, after I heard of your faith in the Lord Jesus, and love unto all the saints, Cease not to give thanks for you, making mention of you in my prayers"* (Ephesians 1:15–16).

Paul said something similar to the church in Thessalonica: *"We give thanks to God always for you all, making mention of you in our prayers"* (1 Thessalonians 1:2). There is a reason that Paul was so careful to mention that he was giving thanks for those whom he prayed for. When God called Paul to pray for and disciple others, Paul made giving thanks for those people a great priority. There is a reason that Scripture speaks of prayer so often in conjunction with thanksgiving. Even if we do not understand all the reasons why, we should take note of the fact that there is power in giving thanks for those for whom we pray. *"Continue in prayer, and watch in the same with thanksgiving"* (Colossians 4:2).

Most of us have probably read God's command to "watch and pray." The concept of watching and praying is familiar and we recognize its importance. How often do we think about what it looks like to watch and pray? How do we learn to do that? One aspect of continuing and watching in prayer is giving thanks! It is easy to come to the Lord in prayer filled with complaints, but God has specifically noted that we are to watch and pray with *thanksgiving*. Maybe you have prayed for a specific person or situation for many years and are seeing no change. Perhaps you are tempted to become bitter with the Lord for seeming to not answer your prayer, or you are becoming discouraged and no longer wanting to continue in watching and praying. Do not give up! Instead of becoming bitter or discouraged, I encourage you to offer to God prayers filled with words of thankfulness to Him. After all, since it is God's will for us to give thanks in everything, we can be sure that to speak to Him with words of thankfulness is part of His will for our prayer life.

When we begin prayer with thanksgiving, we come before the throne of God with gratefulness in our hearts. We enter His gates with thanksgiving and His courts with praise. Giving thanks builds our faith as it ushers us into the presence of the One Who can do the impossible. As we give thanks to God for Who He is and all He has done for us, we are reminded of His faithfulness and of how we can pray with confidence in His care and ability. Times of prayer are not supposed to be times of focusing on ourselves and our problems, but incredible times of fellowship with God as we focus on Who He is, give thanks to Him, and bring others before Him in prayer.

If we are abiding in God's Word, if we are meditating on it day and night and allowing it to become our belief system, we have been given a wonderful guarantee from our Heavenly Father. He guarantees that whatever we ask of Him according to His will, He will give to us. *"If ye abide in me, and my words abide in you, ye shall ask what ye will, and it shall be done unto you"* (John 15:7).

There is so much more that could be said about meditating on God's Word and prayer, but for now, let's focus on something that is a part of receiving what we ask in prayer. We have discovered that our belief system determines our behavior. For example, if we meditate on something, it becomes what we believe and therefore affects what we do. This principle is true in regard to prayer as well. What we think about prayer affects how we pray and also affects what happens after we pray.

Let me explain. When someone hands you a birthday present, what is your response? Most likely, you reach out, accept the gift, and say, "Thank you!" to the one who gave it. Why do you say thank you? Because you believe that the person handing you the wrapped box is giving you something. If you do not believe they are giving you a gift, you will not say thank you, and you will not accept the gift.

When we come before the Lord with our requests and petitions, we need to believe that He is truly going to fulfill His promises and answer our prayers. Even if we do not see yet how He has fulfilled our request, if we say "thank you" to the Lord, we are acting by faith on the truth that He said He will give us what we ask. As we give thanks to the Lord, our faith is built up and we are able to receive answers to prayer. If someone handed me a birthday present and I took it without saying thank you, that would be very rude. Yet how often do we stop to thank God instead of listing our endless requests? Stopping to say thank you is living in humility before God, and it is the expression of a heart that truly believes God answers prayer. I can think of few more convincing signs of faith than giving thanks. To give thanks is taking hold of God's promises whether we feel them or not. It is a part of expressing our belief in God and His promises no matter how things appear. Perhaps we do not *feel* like God has heard our prayers, but that does not change the fact that He has commanded us to give thanks in prayer anyway. The result of this thanksgiving—that began as an act of obedience—often becomes a spontaneous expression of the faith that giving thanks helped to build. How can we *not* thank God when we see His faithfulness, His goodness, His love, and His willingness to hear and answer our prayers? When we pray, we have the confidence that the Lord will answer our prayers if we are abiding in Him and if we have His word abiding in us. Therefore, let us by faith thank the Lord for giving us what we have prayed for, even before we see the answer in the physical realm. Perhaps we sometimes worry because it seems that our prayers are not being answered and that we are not praying with faith. If this is the case, we need to not only meditate on God's Word and make certain that we are asking according to His will, but we also need to begin giving thanks to Him when we pray, just as He has commanded us to. Saying thank you to the Lord is a good way to begin, continue in, and conclude prayer. After all, if we are giving thanks in everything, does not that include giving thanks the whole time we are praying?

George Müller, living in nineteenth century Bristol, England, is an astounding example of living a life of faith-filled prayer. What did his prayers look like? George Müller ran orphanages by faith. This meant that he built homes for orphans and cared for them and trusted God to provide the necessary expenses. Instead of going out to raise funds, Müller would pray. He would go before God in prayer and simply ask God to supply what was needed. God answered those faith-filled prayers and provided in such miraculous ways that the accounts of His faithfulness in Müller's life have continued to bless readers to this day.

At one time, Müller's orphanages housed three hundred orphans. It was during this time that the orphans and staff sat down at the table for a meal and found themselves in an unusual predicament. The tables were set with plates, but there was no food on the plates! The orphanage was completely out of food. George Müller was not worried. He had prayed that God would supply food. Confident that God would provide, Müller led the group in a prayer of thanksgiving. He did not wait until he could see the food; he simply thanked God in faith that He would provide for their needs.

Just then, a knock sounded at the orphanage door. God was at work. The man at the door explained that he was a local baker and that God had prompted him to make bread early that morning and bring it to the orphans. God provided just as Müller had faith that He would! The orphans joyfully received this gift that Müller had already given thanks for.

However, God was not finished demonstrating His power. In a few moments, another knock sounded at the door. This time it was the milkman. His milk cart had broken down in front of the orphanage, he explained, and since the milk in his cart would spoil before he could repair it, he was wondering if the orphanage could use the milk. God supplied milk as well as bread for the thankful orphanage.

George Müller knew that God would provide all his needs and that God would answer his prayers. He believed, and the result of his belief system was an act of faith, thanking God for the food that he knew God would provide. He gave thanks by faith.

Scripture says that the testimonies of the Lord are sure, making wise the simple. (See Psalm 19:7.) Hearing testimonies of the faithfulness of God encourages us to give thanks in prayer. Scripture has another powerful testimony of a man who gave thanks to God in difficult circumstances.

Daniel was brought from Judah to Babylon as a captive when he was a young man. His determination to remain faithful to the Lord, whatever the cost, was honored by God. God gave Daniel great wisdom and favor. In time, Daniel was set over the whole realm of King Darius. The other presidents and princes became jealous of him and set out to find fault with him. Even though they tried hard, they could find no fault in this faithful servant of God. His life was so upright that their only criticism was that he was faithful in prayer. These wicked men told the king to *"establish a royal statute, and make a firm decree, that whosoever shall ask a petition of any God or man for thirty days, save of thee, O king, he shall be cast into the dens of lions"* (Daniel 6:7b). King Darius agreed and signed the petition.

What was Daniel's response when he found out that he would be killed for praying? His response provides us with a powerful key in learning to walk by faith and pray with power. *"Now when Daniel knew that the writing was signed, he went into his house; and his windows being open in his chamber toward Jerusalem, he kneeled upon his knees three times a day, and prayed, and **gave thanks** before his God, as he did aforetime"* (Daniel 6:10, emphasis added).

What an incredible response! Little wonder Daniel was able to stand by his convictions regardless of the cost and even faced a lions' den without fear. His secret was prayer, but not just any prayer; his prayer was infused with thanksgiving. Every day, three times a day, Daniel was in the habit of entering the presence of his Lord with thanksgiving. Even after finding out about the king's edict making prayer punishable with death, Daniel continued. I can picture Daniel throwing open his window, falling to his knees, and giving thanks to the Lord instead of complaining or pouring out fear.

Daniel faced lions. What do we face? Perhaps we feel as if we are confronting our own den of lions: trials, difficulties, fears, or obstacles that seem that insurmountable. Perhaps we shrink from prayer, not fearing a lions' den, but dreading boredom or not knowing what to say. We should respond like Daniel and come before God with prayers filled with thanksgiving.

Have you ever noticed that when you finally set aside time to pray, every worry or trial that has ever beset you seems to rush at you at that moment like a tidal wave? How do we combat this attack from the enemy? We would do well if we followed Daniel's example in such times: get down on our knees and enter the presence of God with thanksgiving. Let every impending lions' den, anxiety, and worry urge us to even more prayer and thanksgiving.

I have discovered that when I begin prayer with giving thanks to my Lord, the otherwise smothering worries and anxieties dissipate like snow under the warm rays of sunlight. There is great power in giving thanks—more power than we have even begun to glimpse.

Let us begin, without delay, to enter the presence of the Lord with thanksgiving and to gaze in wonder at the incredible things He will do as a result! Long before Daniel ever reached the point where he faced a lions' den, he already was in the habit of trusting God. He cultivated it through much time on his knees in prayer and thanksgiving. You and I must begin today, right now, to meditate on the Word of God, to pray to Him, and to give thanks. We must learn this lesson now if we are going to give thanks in the face of lions, as Daniel did. Just as God delivered Daniel from the mouths of lions, He is able to deliver you and I and cause His will to be fulfilled.

Another valuable aspect of prayer is giving thanks to the name of the Lord. Many Scriptures give specific instructions to not merely give thanks generally, but to give thanks to the name of the Lord. 1 Chronicles 16:35 reads, *"And say ye, Save us, O God of our salvation, and gather us together, and deliver us from the heathen, that we may give thanks to thy holy name, and glory in thy praise."*

Perhaps one of the reasons that giving thanks to the name of the Lord is powerful is that the name of the Lord is unchanging. As we talked about earlier, the sovereignty and goodness of God are unchanging reasons for thanksgiving and praise. When we meditate on the names of the Lord by giving thanks unto His Name, we come to recognize that no matter what we are experiencing in life, our God is unchanging! David says in 2 Samuel 22:50, *"Therefore I will give thanks unto thee, O LORD, among the heathen, and I will sing praises unto thy name."*

As believers, we should be the most grateful people on earth. When you and I give thanks to the name of the Lord, we are recognizing our covenant with Him. We are turning our attention to the One Who has committed Himself to fulfill the responsibility of providing for and sustaining us. When we give thanks unto the name of the Lord, we are recognizing Him as a good God Who is faithful to keep His covenant with His children.

And whatsoever ye do in word or deed, do all in
the name of the Lord Jesus, giving thanks to God
and the Father by him (Colossians 3:17).

This verse in Colossians talks about giving thanks, but
it also talks about doing everything in the name of our Lord
Jesus. What does it mean to do things "in His name"? It means
far more than simply saying "in Jesus' name" at the end of a
prayer. Doing things in the name of Jesus speaks of a relationship with God that permeates every area of our lives.

For example, a husband and wife are in covenant. They
share the same last name and are free to do things in the
other spouse's name. Suppose a wife makes a reservation at
a restaurant. When asked whose name to put the reservation
under, she is free to reply with her husband's name. Why can
she do this? Since she is in a covenant with her husband, they
become one. She does things in his name because she has
taken his name as her own. In the same way, if you and I are
in covenant with God through Jesus Christ, we should do all
things in His name. We should live as those who are one with
Him through a covenant relationship and do everything in the
light of the relationship.

A covenant, like a marriage, has a lot of implications.
Not only is there a name change but also a change in identity.
We become one with the other party of the covenant, and
every area of our life is transformed. When a husband and wife
enter into a covenant with each other on their wedding day,
that covenant permeates every area of their life. From that day
forward, every decision they make, every deed they do, and
every word they speak has an effect on their covenant partner.

In the same way, as believers in the Lord Jesus Christ, we have entered into a covenant with the living God, and that means every area of our lives must be affected by that covenant. Everything we do, in word or deed, should be a reflection of the God we have been made one with. One way to show that Christ's life has permeated our life is by giving thanks. Everything we do, in word or in deed, should be done with thanksgiving.

Have you ever wondered why people often give thanks before eating a meal? In the ancient times, when people were going to make a covenant with each other, they often would share a meal together as part of making the covenant. We still have remnants of this in our culture today in that we share a meal with those whom we want to get to know better, people in our family, friends, or business associates. We see in Scripture Jesus giving thanks before He broke bread, and this makes sense when looked at in the light of covenant. Eating a meal is a part of participating in a relationship. Every time you and I partake of a meal, we are doing so as those who are in covenant with Christ. It makes perfect sense to pause before we eat a meal in order to give thanks to our Covenant Partner Who provided it and to recognize His presence with us. Ephesians 5:20 says, *"Giving thanks always for all things unto God and the Father in the name of our Lord Jesus Christ[.]"*

As we give thanks to the name of the Lord and remember that we are also *within* His name, we begin to receive more of the rich abundance that God has provided for us in Christ. Are we weak? We can give thanks in the name of the Lord Jehovah in Whom is everlasting strength. We can recognize Who He is and that we share His name and His strength. That is a name worthy of praise! Are we depressed? Let us give thanks to Him in Whose presence is fullness of joy. Are we insecure? Let us give thanks to Our Deliverer. Are we anxious? Let us give thanks unto the Prince of Peace. As we offer up thanks to God because of Who He is in His eternal nature, and as we remember that we are in Him and He is in us, our lives begin to resonate with the proper tone of a true believer, which is thanksgiving.

Giving thanks is not merely a nice idea. It is part of God's instructions to those of us who have entered an eternal covenant with Him. It is a joyous privilege and an unchanging responsibility.

> The name of the LORD is a strong tower: the righteous runneth into it, and is safe. (Proverbs 18:10)

Whatever we are going through in life, whatever trials we are facing, whatever fears we have, God calls us to run into His name that is a mighty fortress. His name describes His character, and He never changes! As we go to the Lord in prayer and begin magnifying Who God is and what He has done, then, like Daniel, we are safe no matter what we are facing. We discover, no matter how many lions crouch in the way, that we are safe within Him and have unceasing reason to be filled with praise and thanksgiving. Indeed, what an honor and privilege it is to come before the throne of God to give thanks to His glorious name!

CHAPTER EIGHT

THE SACRIFICE OF THANKSGIVING

THROUGHOUT THE OLD Testament Scriptures we find references to the various sacrifices that God's people were commanded to offer. These sacrifices included the burnt offerings and peace offerings. These were part of God's covenant with His people and were pictures of Christ.

One of these was the thanksgiving sacrifice. We discover a powerful principle in God's description of the thanksgiving sacrifice. The thanksgiving sacrifice was a type of peace offering.

> And this is the law of the sacrifice of peace offerings, which he shall offer unto the LORD. If he offer it for a thanksgiving, then he shall offer with the sacrifice of thanksgiving unleavened cakes mingled with oil, and unleavened wafers anointed with oil, and cakes mingled with oil, of fine flour, fried. (Leviticus 7:11–12)

The thanksgiving sacrifice was a part of God's desire to walk in relationship with His people and to give them peace. Thanksgiving and peace are closely linked. When you and I come before the Lord offering Him the sacrifice of praise by giving thanks, His peace begins to rule in our hearts and minds. In a sense, thanksgiving is a sacrifice that we give to God, and peace is something that He offers us in return. Philippians 4:6–7 says, *"Be careful for nothing; but in every thing by prayer and supplication with thanksgiving let your requests be made known unto God. And the peace of God, which passeth all understanding, shall keep your hearts and minds through Christ Jesus."*

When faced with a difficulty or problem as was mentioned earlier, we have two choices. We can either worry and complain, or we can choose, by God's grace, to bring the situations and difficulties before the Lord in prayer and give thanks in the midst of those things. The first option ends in despair. Our problems seem to grow and we find ourselves in constant turmoil. The second option is the only choice for the followers of Jesus. The result of offering the sacrifice of thanksgiving to God is that His peace rules in our hearts.

What causes so many believers to walk around in a fog of confusion, fear, and anxiety instead of the peace that Christ has purchased for us? Usually, it is because we are stepping outside the jurisdiction that God has assigned to us. He has given us our responsibility: to trust Him, to pray, and to thank Him. When you and I step outside of that jurisdiction and complain and worry, we find that we lack peace. This is only logical, because in stepping outside of our jurisdiction, we have refused the peace of God. However, there is hope! When we remain within the boundaries of God's commands to us by giving thanks instead of complaining, praying instead of worrying, and so forth, we experience the astoundingly refreshing peace that God offers to those who will allow His peace to rule in their hearts. Part of living under the reign of God's peace requires offering the sacrifice of thanksgiving. Colossians 3:15 says, *"And let the peace of God rule in your hearts, to the which also ye are called in one body; and be ye thankful."*

Letting the peace of God rule our hearts is not a suggestion; it is a command. When we are thankful, the peace of God rules our hearts. If we desire peace from God, we must be willing to offer the sacrifice of thanksgiving.

Why is thanksgiving identified as a sacrifice? What if we do not feel thankful when we come before God? Isn't it hypocritical to say "Thank You" to the Lord and to praise Him if we do not feel thankful or joyful? It is easy to wonder whether our thanksgiving to the Lord is even a pleasing sacrifice to Him when we know all too well the cold, ungrateful disposition of our wicked heart. I believe that the answer to these questions can be found in the very simple understanding of what a sacrifice is. A sacrifice is an offering of the will.

And when ye will offer a sacrifice of thanksgiving unto the Lord, offer it at your own will. (Leviticus 22:29)

An act of the will is performed outside of the realm of emotions. For example, good parents with a young baby often need to get up in the middle of the night to feed and care for their infant. They do not get up in the middle of the night because they *feel* like it or enjoy being awakened; they sacrifice sleep and pleasure as an act of their will for the sake of their little one.

As human beings, our emotions are ever changing. One day we may feel joyful and want to give thanks. The next day we may feel depressed and not have even the slightest desire to give thanks. That is where the wonderful opportunity comes to make a sacrifice of thanksgiving as an act of the will. As we meditate on the Word of God and give Him control over our thoughts and actions, it is possible to watch as He works thanksgiving in our lives by causing us to give thanks even if we do not feel that we want to.

Rest assured that while a lack of thanksgiving in our lives is sin, a lack of thankful feelings is not. God does not want us to wait until we feel thankful before we offer that sacrifice. The word "sacrifice" denotes that we are giving up something. It is easy to offer the sacrifice of thanksgiving to God when we feel like doing so, but when we give thanks even when we do not have grateful emotions, I wonder if that level of sacrifice is even more pleasing to our Lord. By offering the sacrifice of thanksgiving even when we do not feel thankful, we are not being hypocritical, but sacrificial. Thanksgiving is a sacrifice.

As God works in us both to will and to do of His good pleasure, (see Philippians 2:13,) as He works thanksgiving into our lives and hearts, He transforms our attitude in making that sacrifice. While we may not feel thankful, as we thank the Lord anyway, we are offering the sacrifice of thanksgiving. God desires that we offer the sacrifice of thanksgiving not grudgingly, but freely and joyously.

> Every man according as he purposeth in his heart,
> so let him give; not grudgingly, or of necessity: for
> God loveth a cheerful giver. (2 Corinthians 9:7)

God loves a cheerful giver. If giving thanks to God is a sacrifice, we must do so with a cheerful heart. That is the kind of sacrifice that God loves! It is easier to offer our sacrifice cheerfully when we remember that we are thanking the God Who is good and Who is in control. As we meditate on the truth of Who God is and what He is working in our lives even through suffering, we are strengthened to give thanks cheerfully.

Another fascinating aspect of the thanksgiving offering described in Leviticus is that the flesh of the sacrifice had to be eaten the same day it was offered; none of the sacrifice was to be left for the next day.

> And the flesh of the sacrifice of his peace offerings
> for thanksgiving shall be eaten the same day that
> it is offered; he shall not leave any of it until the
> morning. (Leviticus 7:15)

Perhaps you and I gave thanks yesterday or before our last meal and assume that is enough. Thanksgiving is not a one-time offering. You and I cannot "coast along" on yesterday's giving of thanks. The giving of thanks is to be a continual sacrifice that we offer to the Lord moment by moment whether we feel like it or not.

This makes perfect sense in the light of the fact that giving thanks is a part of entering God's presence, walking in relationship with Him, and seeing His will fulfilled in our lives. We should never leave God's presence or cease to seek Him and His will for our lives. So we must never cease to offer the sacrifice of thanksgiving! If we gave thanks yesterday, praise God for that; however, that does not exempt us from offering the sacrifice of thanksgiving again today. The sacrifice of thanksgiving is continuous and joyous.

Another truth that we see in the description of God's requirements for the thanksgiving offering is that even though the sacrifice was offered to the Lord, the individual who made the sacrifice was the one who ate and left nourished and strengthened. When we offer to God the sacrifice of praise by giving thanks to Him, as we let go of our own wills and surrender to God's requirements, we are not weakened. Instead, we are strengthened just as those who offered the sacrifice of thanksgiving were nourished by their sacrifice. Thanksgiving is a sacrifice, but it is rewarded with the nourishment of the peace and presence of the Lord. In a sense, thanksgiving is more of a gift than a sacrifice because in offering the sacrifice of thanksgiving, we receive indescribable riches in return!

David makes an incredibly powerful and eye-opening statement in Psalm 69 after talking about the hardship and sorrow that he was going through.

I will praise the name of God with a song and will magnify Him with thanksgiving. This also shall please the Lord more than an ox or bullock that hath horns and hooves. (Psalm 69:30–31)

In David's time, oxen and bullocks were both valued animals. When an individual brought oxen or bullocks to the Lord, they were making a significant sacrifice. They were surrendering animals that were valued as work animals as well as food. What is something important in your life that is considered valuable? Your car? Your house or bank account? Those things are valuable in the earthly sense, just as oxen and bullocks were valuable in David's time. You may say, "I will offer my car and house and bank account to God!

I will sacrifice those to Him." That is wonderful! That is exactly what God calls us to do—to give everything in our lives over to Him. But what about the sacrifice of thanksgiving? God does desire that we surrender things such as our money and possessions to Him, but I wonder if we are often willing to sacrifice those things to Him before we are willing to offer the sacrifice of thanksgiving. We think of giving thanks as second rate—as something that we will offer to God if we get around to it. Surely God is more interested in "bigger" sacrifices than merely my giving thanks to Him! Yet David said that praising and magnifying God *with thanksgiving* would be more pleasing to the Lord than an ox or bullock.

Could it be that the world, the flesh, and the devil are intent on minimizing the importance of giving thanks because the giving of thanks is one of the very things that God deeply desires from us? Giving thanks is an important part of walking in relationship with the Lord, walking in humility before Him, and entering His presence. That is the kind of sacrifice that God is eager for us to make! Sometimes it is easy to offer "big" things to God, but far more difficult to surrender our thoughts to Him by meditating on His Word, our mouths to Him by speaking thanksgiving instead of complaining, and our days to thankful prayer instead of seeking self. Thanksgiving is a sacrifice that requires us to take our eyes off ourselves and to humble ourselves before the Lord. It is a sacrifice that pleases Him more than the sacrifice of the ox or a bullock. Since we were created for the purpose of pleasing the Lord, let us, by His grace, in addition to surrendering our prized possessions, cheerfully offer Him the sacrifice He desires: that of thanksgiving.

The sacrifice of thanksgiving is intertwined with our words. To offer our hearts, and therefore our words, to the Lord is the substance of the sacrifice of thanksgiving. *"By him therefore let us offer the sacrifice of praise to God continually, that is, the fruit of our lips giving thanks to his name"* (Hebrews 13:15).

God describes thanksgiving as fruit. A fruit-bearing vine, such as a grape vine, bears fruit naturally. Fruit is a result of the life found in the source of that fruit. Christ is our True Vine. As we abide in Him and His Word abides in us, praise and thanksgiving are a part of the fruit of His life in us. Thanksgiving is a willful sacrifice, but that willful sacrifice is the result of the power of Jesus in us causing us to bear, and offer, the fruit of thanksgiving. *"I am the vine, ye are the branches: he that abideth in me, and I in him, the same bringeth forth much fruit: for without me ye can do nothing"* (John 15:5).

If we want to offer the sacrifice of thanksgiving to God, we must be full of the Word of God. Only God's Word living in us will bring forth the fruit of thanksgiving. If we are meditating on what we want, what we are not getting, and so on, then the fruit of our lips will be murmuring and complaining. On the other hand, if we abide in God's Word and His Word abides in us, we become so full of joy and gratitude that we cannot help but bring forth the fruit of giving thanks. The sacrifice of thanksgiving is a willful choice that we make only as our will is exchanged for the will of God by abiding in Him and meditating on His Word. *"These things have I spoken unto you, that my joy might remain in you, and that your joy might be full"* (John 15:11).

A truly joyful heart filled with praise and bearing the fruit of thanksgiving comes as a result of abiding in the Word of God, of meditating on it continually. As you and I meditate day and night upon God's Word, God fills us with His joy, and the fruit of our lips becomes thankfulness to Him.

An example of offering the sacrifice of thanksgiving can be found in the extraordinary account of Jonah. God called to Jonah *"Arise, go to Nineveh, that great city, and cry against it; for their wickedness is come up before me"* (Jonah 1:2). Instead of obeying the voice of the Lord, Jonah attempted to flee from His presence and boarded a ship bound for Tarshish.

While they were at sea, a raging tempest came up. Jonah realized that the reason the storm came upon them was because he sinned against the Lord by not going to Nineveh. Jonah told the crew of the ship *"...Take me up, and cast me forth into the sea; so shall the sea be calm unto you: for I know that for my sake this great tempest is upon you"* (Jonah 1:12).

Before they listened to God's prophet, they tried to fix this situation their own way by rowing harder. It did not work. So, reluctantly, the crew did as Jonah asked and threw him overboard. Immediately the storm was calm. *"Now the LORD had prepared a great fish to swallow up Jonah. And Jonah was in the belly of the fish three days and three nights"* (Jonah 1:17).

Most of us are very familiar with the account of Jonah. We hear about his fleeing from the Lord, his confinement in the belly of the fish, and the rest of his story. Often, we forget what happened to Jonah while he was in the midst of the belly of the fish. Jonah cried out to God. He offered the sacrifice of thanksgiving.

Then Jonah prayed unto the Lord his God out of the fish's belly, And said, I cried by reason of mine affliction unto the LORD, and he heard me; out of the belly of hell cried I, and thou heardest my voice. For thou hadst cast me into the deep, in the midst of the seas; and the floods compassed me about: all thy billows and thy waves passed over me. Then I said, I am cast out of thy sight; yet I will look again toward thy holy temple. The waters compassed me about, even to the soul: the depth closed me round about, the weeds were wrapped about my head. I went down to the bottoms of the mountains; the earth with her bars was about me for ever: yet hast thou brought up my life from corruption, O LORD my God. When my soul fainted within me I remembered the LORD: and my prayer came in unto thee, into thine holy temple. They that observe lying vanities forsake their own mercy. But I will **sacrifice unto thee with the voice of thanksgiving;** I will pay that that I have vowed. Salvation is of the LORD. (Jonah 2:1–9, emphasis added)

Imagine where Jonah was when he prayed this prayer! Imagine the slime and sludge that surrounded him, the horrific stench, and the fearful, enclosed darkness that must have seemed to smother him. Those of us who have cleaned a fish know how messy and disgusting it can be; imagine living inside of one! Imagine how Jonah must have had to gasp for breath and try to avoid the partially digested food that crowded in upon him. It was in the midst of this horrible, terrifying, and perhaps claustrophobic environment that Jonah gave thanks.

As He did with Jonah, God will often bring us to the end of ourselves in the midst of challenging and at times even dark seasons, in order to teach us our greatest lessons. Like Jonah, sometimes we walk in pride and rebel against God when He is leading us to go one way and we turn the opposite way. Frequently, His response is to allow trials into our lives in order to draw us back to Himself. Just as God brought the fish to Jonah, He will allow difficult circumstances that seem to swallow us up and bring us to despair of ourselves. Jonah's response to his time in the belly of the great fish was to offer the sacrifice of thanksgiving. He did not wait until circumstances were more pleasant or for positive feelings to flow over him before he offered the fruit of his lips in order to give thanks to God. Instead, in the midst of the fish's belly, shrouded in oppressive darkness, Jonah turned to the Lord in prayer and, specifically, a prayer of thanksgiving. Sometimes the most unlikely of places can become our prayer closet; in Jonah's case, his prayer closet was the belly of a fish!

After the fish spit Jonah out and he obeyed the voice of the Lord and went to Nineveh, we see that Jonah still had much to learn about thankfulness and true love. The Lord still used him powerfully in Nineveh, and that was after Jonah offered the sacrifice of thanksgiving. God desires to fulfill His will in our lives in incredible ways, and our responsibility, in agreement with His will, is to offer the sacrifice of thanksgiving before our circumstances change. We see yet again that the sacrifice of thanksgiving is to be a continual sacrifice.

Giving thanks always and in all things, even in the belly of a fish, requires true sacrifice. It means letting go of our wills, our complaints, and our discontentment and instead offering the sacrifice of thanksgiving that truly pleases God. As we offer the sacrifice, God fills us with joy and gives us grace and strength to handle the trial we are going through. Are we, like Jonah, entangled with weeds, crushed with darkness, and feeling trapped? Now is our opportunity to offer the sacrifice of thanksgiving. Let us not wait for the opportunity to pass. The sacrifice of thanksgiving is a continual offering.

CHAPTER NINE

GIVING THANKS
IN SUFFERING

GIVING THANKS TO the Lord in everything includes both times of suffering and times of joy. This basic truth is one that many of us can be quick to forget. As we obediently give thanks to the Lord during trials and suffering, we bring pleasure to the heart of God and our lives are a testimony to a dying world of the power of the living God. People who do not know God have no reason to rejoice in suffering. Our knowledge of God should cause us to give thanks, and thereby reveal to the world that our God is living and that He is worthy of all praise and thanksgiving. Giving thanks in suffering is a sign to the world that our God is the God of hope. Thanksgiving in everything is a living testimony.

Trials do not seem good, they do not look good, and they most certainly do not feel good! However, if we love God and are called according to His purpose, suffering and pain are used by God to fulfill His purpose for our lives. We can joyfully thank the Lord even in the midst of pain and difficulty because we know that God is using those trials to empty us of ourselves—of our own self-confidence, selfishness, and pride—and to fill us with His patience, His love—with His very self. This means that contrary to how we feel and how situations may appear, suffering is used by God for good. In fact, as we learn to see life from God's perspective, we can begin to embrace His working in us through suffering. This sounds impossible at first, but the truth is that if you and I fully understood the incredible work that God does in our lives through suffering, we would embrace suffering as something that is used by God to conform us to the image of His Son.

Before continuing to share about how God uses suffering, I would like to clarify some important points to keep in mind. I am not saying that God created suffering or that He wants His children to suffer. Suffering and pain came as a result of the fall. (See Genesis 3:14–19.) Through man's choice to rebel against God, sin entered the world and brought with it suffering, pain, and death. (See Romans 5:12.) Scripture says that, as a result of the fall, the whole of creation groans and travails in pain. (See Romans 8:22.) Death, decay, and suffering were not part of God's original, good creation.

Scripture is also very clear that God can even take what Satan meant for evil and use it for such incredible good that we can recognize God's blessing even in the midst of the most challenging difficulties. (See Genesis 50:20.) Romans 5:20b reads, *"But where sin abounded, grace did much more abound."* I believe that just like where sin abounds grace much more abounds, where the effects of sin abound grace can abound as well. As we face the suffering and pain that are a result of the fall, we can know in a special way the *super*-abounding grace of God. We can know that He can use the difficulty to burn off the dross in our lives and shape us into His image.

There are countless examples of how God brings good out of evil. The greatest time we see this is at the cross. Jesus, the perfect, holy Son of God was taken by sinful man and slain. That was a grave sin. In John 13:2, we read how the devil put it in the heart of Judas Iscariot to betray Jesus. The devil wanted to destroy the Son of God, and yet, God's purpose was accomplished through the cross. Satan thought that he won a victory against God; Jesus actually used the cross to defeat Satan! (See Hebrews 2:14–15.) God brought the greatest good out of the worst evil. Although our suffering is not the same (Jesus suffered once for all to bring redemption to mankind— see Hebrews 10:10), God can work to bring good out of evil in the situations in our lives.

The world around us, and the sinful nature within us, does not naturally believe that suffering can be something beneficial; we do not naturally believe that trials serve a purpose. This means that we need our minds to be renewed; we need to know that the trying of our faith works patience. Again, we see that what we meditate on determines what we believe about suffering and therefore determines how we will respond to that suffering. The more we meditate on the truth about suffering, the more it becomes possible for us to surrender to the Lord's use of suffering in our lives and to give thanks to Him in the midst of that suffering. Giving thanks in everything, just like walking in obedience to the Lord in any other area, is the result of receiving the power of God, and receiving the truth through meditation on God's Word.

Suffering is part of God's plan to make us His heirs. Romans 8:17 says, *"And if children, then heirs; heirs of God, and joint-heirs with Christ; if so be that we suffer with him, that we may be also glorified together.*" When we rejoice in suffering, God is glorified in us. As you and I suffer, we are becoming joint-heirs with Christ. Suffering, although it may often appear difficult and perhaps without purpose, is actually God's means of burning off the dross in our lives so that Christ can be seen more clearly through us. We may not understand why God uses suffering as His vehicle for this incredible goal, but the fact is that He does. We can be grateful, even in the midst of suffering, because the life of Christ being seen within us is worth the suffering God uses in order to shape us into vessels through which He can work.

> For I reckon that the sufferings of this present
> time are not worthy to be compared with the glory
> which shall be revealed in us. (Romans 8:18)

We are to rejoice in our sufferings for Christ's sake. Paul says in 2 Corinthians 4:8–10, *"We are troubled on every side, yet not distressed; we are perplexed, but not in despair; Persecuted, but not forsaken; cast down, but not destroyed; Always bearing about in the body the dying of the Lord Jesus, that the life also of Jesus might be made manifest in our body."*

We are to always bear about in our body the dying of the Lord Jesus, and this can happen through suffering. Suffering is an opportunity for us to die to self and see the life of Jesus made manifest in our bodies. Meditating on this truth opens up to us the reason to embrace suffering, in order that Christ might live through us.

Giving thanks in our suffering is a very effective way to embrace the suffering instead of resisting it and becoming bitter. As we begin to understand the truth about suffering, we can see how God is working through it to accomplish His purpose in our lives. We often may not be able to immediately comprehend the purpose in our present suffering, but we can be sure that if we are suffering for the sake of Christ, God is working something important in us through it; we are being emptied of ourselves in order that we might be filled with His Life.

> That the **trial of your faith,** being much more **precious than of gold** that perisheth, though it be tried with fire, might be found unto praise and honour and glory at the appearing of Jesus Christ: (1 Peter 1:7, emphasis added)

What greater treasure could we possibly desire more than faith? Without faith it is impossible to please God. In order to try our faith, in order to perfect in us that which will enable us to please Him, God allows suffering in our lives. Do we value pleasing God more than we value being comfortable? If we do, and if we understand that the life of Christ being formed in us is part of the end goal in suffering, then we would conclude that the suffering we so quickly complain about is worth more than gold. The fact is, if someone offered us a choice between receiving a million dollars or the eternal work God would do in our lives through receiving suffering with thanksgiving, we would do well to choose God's work in us through suffering above even great riches.

This is a difficult truth for us to grapple with, but as we understand and meditate on the value of suffering, we can begin to receive it with the same joy and thanksgiving with which we would receive great riches. This illustrates again how it is only through meditating on God's Word that the fruit of thankfulness is displayed in our lives. The only way you and I are going to sincerely embrace suffering with thanksgiving is if we are abiding in Christ, receiving His Word through meditating upon it, and no longer resisting Him as He forms His thankfulness in us.

God's plan to form the life of Christ in us often includes suffering in our lives. One reason God uses suffering as His tool for this purpose is because when we are suffering in the flesh, we cease from sin. God uses suffering to burn off the dross from our lives and so to purify us and make us fit vessels for the Master's use.

> Forasmuch then as Christ hath suffered for us in the flesh, arm yourselves likewise with the same mind: for he that hath suffered in the flesh hath ceased from sin; (1 Peter 4:1)

If we are going to arm ourselves with the same mind that Christ had when He suffered, we must think the thoughts of Christ; we must meditate on His Word. As we do so, we are receiving His mind on the subject of suffering and are walking in the footsteps of Christ. What reason do we have to give thanks for suffering? One reason is because we are ceasing from sin. Another is that it is an opportunity to walk in the steps of Christ—to follow our Lord where He walked.

> For even hereunto were ye called: because Christ also suffered for us, leaving us an example, that ye should follow his steps: (1 Peter 2:21)

We should also realize that sometimes God uses suffering to chasten us. Hebrews 12:6 reveals that one of the ways our Heavenly Father expresses His love for us is through discipline: *"For whom the Lord loveth he chasteneth, and scourgeth every son whom he receiveth."* 1 Peter 2:20 highlights the fact that sometimes our suffering can be a result of our wrong choices or sin: *"For what glory is it, if, when ye be buffeted for your faults, ye shall take it patiently? but if, when ye do well, and suffer for it, ye take it patiently, this is acceptable with God."*

In light of this, when suffering or persecution comes our way, we need to go to God, and ask Him to search our hearts, like the Psalmist said: *"Search me, O God, and know my heart: try me, and know my thoughts: And see if there be any wicked way in me, and lead me in the way everlasting"* (Psalm 139:23–24). We want God to show us whether we are suffering for righteousness or because of our own wrongdoing. If God exposes sin in our life, we should confess and forsake it. We can then give thanks to the Lord for using the difficulty to purify us and conform us to the image of His Son.

What if we are doing what is right and yet, are suffering? What if we are persecuted by other people for following what God has commanded? How can we give thanks under those circumstances? We can give thanks when we suffer for doing what is right because we know that if we are being persecuted for the sake of the Lord, this is a sign that, by God's grace, we are living godly in Christ Jesus! Even if we do not feel or see any good in the persecution that we are experiencing, we can always rejoice because the very persecution itself is proof that God's promises are unbroken. He promised in 2 Timothy 3:12, *"Yea, and all that will live godly in Christ Jesus shall suffer persecution."*

We can rest assured that our suffering for the sake of Christ is not in vain! *"But the God of all grace, who hath called us unto his eternal glory by Christ Jesus, after that ye have suffered a while, make you perfect, stablish, strengthen, settle you"* (1 Peter 5:10). Let us give thanks in all things, especially in suffering, because we know our God, and we know that He is using that suffering for His purposes. *"For unto you it is given in the behalf of Christ, not only to believe on him, but also to suffer for his sake;"* (Philippians 1:29).

The early disciples understood that suffering for our Lord is an honor. Peter, who wrote so much about the value of suffering in the book of 1 Peter, was once fearful of suffering. He was so afraid of suffering with the Lord that he denied Jesus three times before the Lord's crucifixion. However, his attitude changed dramatically on the day of Pentecost when the Spirit of the Lord filled Peter. The life of Christ living within Peter made all the difference. Instead of fleeing from suffering and avoiding it at all costs, Peter became as bold as a lion and was willing to suffer for the sake of the Lord. The Spirit of the Lord had to indwell Peter before he could live in the reality of the truth about suffering.

This contrast is seen in the book of Acts when Peter and some of the other apostles were arrested and thrown in jail. During the night, an angel of the Lord came to them and opened the prison doors, instructing them to *"Go, stand and speak in the temple to the people all the words of this life"* (Acts 5:20). Peter and the other apostles knew that if they preached to the people in defiance to the commands of the religious leaders, they would almost certainly be jailed again. Instead of fleeing suffering, Peter and the apostles believed it was an honor to suffer for the

Lord and gladly walked in His steps. (See 1 Peter 2:21.) When the guards came to the prison to fetch them out, they were shocked to find the apostles missing. They had escaped! It was not long before the soldiers found their prisoners preaching openly in the temple about the Lord Jesus Christ.

Peter and the other apostles did endure suffering as a result of their obedience to God. They were re-arrested, severely beaten, and sent away with the stern command to not speak in the name of Jesus. How did the apostles respond to this suffering? Did they complain? Did they seek to escape it? No. They embraced the suffering. *"...and when they had called the apostles, and beaten them, they commanded that they should not speak in the name of Jesus, and let them go. And they departed from the presence of the council, rejoicing that they were counted worthy to suffer shame for his name. And daily in the temple, and in every house, they ceased not to teach and preach Jesus Christ"* (Acts 5:40–42). The apostles responded to the persecution with rejoicing. They understood that suffering for the sake of Christ was a blessing. They understood what Jesus said in Matthew 5:10, *"Blessed are they which are persecuted for righteousness' sake: for theirs is the kingdom of heaven."* It is not enough for us merely to endure persecution; Jesus said that we are to rejoice and be exceeding glad.

> Blessed are ye, when men shall revile you, and persecute you, and shall say all manner of evil against you falsely, for my sake. Rejoice, and be exceeding glad: for great is your reward in heaven: for so persecuted they the prophets which were before you. (Matthew 5:11–12)

Persecution can come in many different forms. Perhaps it may come through slander. Or it may look like being attacked, mocked, or lied about. No matter what form of persecution we are facing, if we are suffering for the sake of Christ, God has called us to receive that persecution with thanksgiving and to rejoice in it. When God commands us to give thanks in everything, *everything* includes suffering and persecution. God does not promise that persecution for Christ's sake will be painless, but He does promise a great reward. He also promises that if we are reproached for the name of Christ, then, on our part, Christ is glorified. As we have already begun to realize, Christ being glorified in us is part of the purpose of our existence. Persecution is something God allows for the accomplishing of His purposes. Let us in everything, even persecution, give thanks.

> If ye be reproached for the name of Christ, happy are ye; for the spirit of glory and of God resteth upon you: on their part he is evil spoken of, but on your part he is glorified. (1 Peter 4:14)

The apostle Paul and his ministry partner Silas also experienced intense suffering and rejoiced in it. One time, after upsetting some rich Macedonians by casting out an unclean spirit, they were severely beaten and thrown into jail. They were considered "important" prisoners and were kept under maximum security. One can almost picture them as they were led into a dimly-lit, damp cell of the inner prison. Their bleeding bodies pulsed with pain and their feet were clamped into unyielding stocks that grasped them with a cruel grip. When we think about their situation from a natural perspective, we would think that these men had every reason to complain.

They were suffering persecution and enduring intense pain, even though they had committed no crime. Perhaps they listened to the screams and groans of their fellow prisoners who also languished in that miserable place.

What Paul and Silas did next could only be explained by the grace of God. They did not complain or cry out in misery; instead, they did something that if you and I also do, our lives will be radically changed. In the middle of the night, at what could have been their lowest point, they began to sing praises to the Lord.

> And at midnight Paul and Silas prayed, and sang praises unto God: and the prisoners heard them. And suddenly there was a great earthquake, so that the foundations of the prison were shaken: and immediately all the doors were opened, and every one's bands were loosed. (Acts 16:25–26)

This is the power of praise! As the ground quaked and the foundations were shaken, the prison doors swung open and the stocks that bound the men fell off. Often we are most tempted to doubt the power and importance of giving thanks and praising the Lord when we are in the midst of suffering and darkness. Yet in their midnight hour, Paul and Silas welcomed the mighty power of God into their situation, not by complaining, but by praise! Our weakest, darkest moments are times in which we need God; we should especially recognize and receive Him by giving thanks and praising Him in those times. There is a reason that God instructs us to give thanks in everything! The midnight hour, in the darkest and seemingly most insurmountable difficulties in our lives, is our opportunity to give thanks and to see the power of God at work. When facing this darkness and discouragement, it is vital for us to humble ourselves and give thanks to God because we need Him so much in those difficult times. Praising God in suffering is part of humbling ourselves and receiving grace to endure and triumph.

Giving thanks in times of suffering both opens the way for God to work in our own lives and also affects the lives of those around us. When Paul and Silas sang God's praises, they saw God work. Not only did both their chains drop off, but everyone around them had their chains fall off too! Death and life are in the power of the tongue. (See Proverbs 18:21.) When you and I speak words of gratefulness to God, when we sing His praises no matter how we feel, others are set free. Giving thanks in everything, even suffering, is not only our duty toward God, but also to our fellow man. Do we yearn for God to break the chains of doubt, fear, and evil from those we love, or from those we see living in sin and despair? It is time that we turn our eyes upon Jesus by giving Him thanks in everything, including suffering, and watch what He will do in the lives of others.

The result of Paul's and Silas' rejoicing in adversity is awe-inspiring. When the jailor saw the life of Christ revealed so clearly through their supernatural rejoicing, he was drawn to the Lord. In fact, he asked Paul and Silas, "Sirs, what must I do to be saved?" (Acts 16:30). When you and I choose, by God's grace, to give thanks in all things, non-believers are drawn to the Lord because they see the life of the Lord—His gratefulness—living in us. There is a reason that when the Lord instructs us to be ready to give an answer, He describes what others will be asking about: they will be asking the reason of the hope that lies within us. A hopeful life should be a hallmark of the believer. (See 1 Peter 3:15.) If we as believers are bogged down in despair and hopelessness, what will the world have to inquire about? Anyone can complain, but only those who live a life hid with Christ in God and see life through His perspective are able to have hope in all circumstances and give thanks to the Lord.

> Do all things without murmurings and disputings: That ye may be blameless and harmless, the sons of God, without rebuke, in the midst of a crooked and perverse nation, among whom ye shine as lights in the world; Holding forth the word of life; that I may rejoice in the day of Christ, that I have not run in vain, neither laboured in vain. (Philippians 2:14–16)

It is possible for us to endure suffering with thankfulness as we remember that Jesus too was described as a Man of Sorrows; He was stricken, smitten, and afflicted for us. He was led as a lamb to the slaughter, willing to suffer, not reviling even when He was reviled. Embracing suffering without complaint is the way of the cross. It is the way that our Master walked, and He has called us to follow in His footsteps. We are called to surrender to His very Life, which is a life of giving thanks.

Christ embraced suffering, and only as we rely completely on His Spirit will we follow in His footsteps. Christ is not only our example in suffering, but He is also our power and grace to endure that suffering. We give thanks because we are crucified with Christ and now the crucified and risen Christ lives in us. *"For even hereunto were ye called: because Christ also suffered for us, leaving us an example, that ye should follow his steps"* (1 Peter 2:21).

One reason we should suffer with thanksgiving is that suffering is a part of the process that we go through in order that the love of God might be shed abroad in our hearts. Even if we can see no earthly value in the suffering we are enduring, we should give thanks that God wants to use that suffering in order to reveal His love to us. Romans 5:4–5 says, *"And not only so, but we glory in tribulations also: knowing that tribulation worketh patience; And patience, experience; and experience, hope: And hope maketh not ashamed; because the love of God is shed abroad in our hearts by the Holy Ghost which is given unto us."* Embracing suffering and tribulation starts a wonderful chain reaction in our lives.

As we begin to glory in tribulation by giving thanks to God and embracing the suffering, we begin to learn patience. This is one of the first things that God desires to produce in our lives through suffering. James 1:2–4 highlights this: *"My brethren, count it all joy when ye fall into divers temptations; Knowing this, that the trying of your faith worketh patience. But let patience have her perfect work, that ye may be perfect and entire, wanting nothing."* We are to count it all joy when facing these various trials because of what we know. We know, according to this verse, that trials work patience. God has a purpose for these trials. Receiving and walking in the patience that God desires for us is a requirement for living in the wholeness that God has planned for us. If we are going to be "perfect and entire, wanting nothing," then we must embrace God's work in us through suffering. Suffering has a purpose and that purpose is worthy of rejoicing in!

God wants to build upon our patience and build experience in our lives. The Greek word translated "experience" in Romans 5:4 holds the idea of something that has been tested, proven, and found trustworthy. We can give thanks in the midst of suffering because God is using that suffering to refine us—to burn away the dross in order that Christ might be more evident in and through our lives.

Rejoicing in God's working in us through suffering is an important part of becoming trustworthy—not that you and I become more trustworthy in ourselves, but that the trustworthy One lives in and through us. Suffering teaches us our own inadequacy and causes us to cast ourselves in total dependence upon the Lord to be our Life, our Righteousness, our All. *His* trustworthiness is worked in us.

As we embrace suffering, the Lord teaches us patience and experience. As we rejoice in the suffering and receive it with thanksgiving, the Lord begins to fill us with hope. If you and I are going to live in hope, then we must suffer. Suffering and hope may at first sound like opposites. However, God says that true hope waits for what it does not see. *"For we are saved by hope: but hope that is seen is not hope: for what a man seeth, why doth he yet hope for? But if we hope for that we see not, then do we with patience wait for it"* (Romans 8:24–25). As you and I embrace suffering with thanksgiving, we learn to respond to the goodness of God even when we do not see how He is working all things together for good.

The result of this faith-filled walk is that we learn to see Christ, the true Reality, instead of seeing our own feelings, doubts, and circumstances. As we look at what cannot be seen, we wait patiently for God to fulfill His purpose and learn more of what it means to live a hope-filled life.

Perhaps we feel as if our suffering is too great and that we have no hope. As we give thanks in the midst of that suffering, turning our focus upon God and His power, instead of responding to situations based on our feelings, we are beginning to walk in hope.

> And not only so, but we glory in tribulations also: knowing that tribulation worketh patience; And patience, experience; and experience, hope: And hope maketh not ashamed; because the love of God is shed abroad in our hearts by the Holy Ghost which is given unto us. (Romans 5:4–5)

Shed abroad means "to pour forth." Here we see part of God's purpose in suffering: that we would be filled with the Holy Spirit and the love of God would be poured forth in our hearts. With this understanding, we cannot help but rejoice in suffering.

This is why Paul gloried in his tribulation. Paul was no stranger to suffering. Lest we mistakenly believe that Paul led an easy life free of trials, we are given a description of his experiences in 2 Corinthians 11:23–30:

> Are they ministers of Christ? (I speak as a fool) I am more; in labours more abundant, in stripes above measure, in prisons more frequent, in deaths oft. Of the Jews five times received I forty stripes save one. Thrice was I beaten with rods, once was

I stoned, thrice I suffered shipwreck, a night and a day I have been in the deep; In journeyings often, in perils of waters, in perils of robbers, in perils by mine own countrymen, in perils by the heathen, in perils in the city, in perils in the wilderness, in perils in the sea, in perils among false brethren; In weariness and painfulness, in watchings often, in hunger and thirst, in fastings often, in cold and nakedness. Beside those things that are without, that which cometh upon me daily, the care of all the churches. Who is weak, and I am not weak? who is offended, and I burn not? If I must needs glory, I will glory of the things which concern mine infirmities.

Paul rejoiced in the midst of such intense suffering because he understood that God was using it to conform him to the image of Christ. Paul so realized the value of suffering that he said that if he must glory, he would glory in things concerning his infirmities. He had such deep insight into the value of suffering and what it produces that he was able to rejoice in the weakness that you and I so often resist. He was able to live a victorious, joyous life even when beaten, stoned, and shipwrecked.

The Lord also allowed a thorn in the flesh to plague Paul. While we do not know what that thorn in the flesh was, we can be sure that it caused suffering for Paul, or it would not have been called a thorn. Why did God allow that thorn? It was in order that Paul would learn to completely depend on the Lord. As he suffered the effects of the thorn in the flesh,

Paul discovered that Christ's grace is sufficient and His power is made perfect in weakness. The life of Christ was made evident in Paul because of the suffering he walked through.

When God allows you and I to suffer, we should give thanks because God uses suffering to teach us to depend on Him and as an opportunity for us to receive His all-sufficient grace. Paul made a statement that we should learn from: *"Therefore I take pleasure in infirmities, in reproaches, in necessities, in persecutions, in distresses for Christ's sake: for when I am weak, then am I strong"* (2 Corinthians 12:10).

When God allows suffering in our lives and shows us our bankruptcy and inability, He is also preparing us to see His ability and strength. Suffering is a tool that God uses to open our eyes, first to who we are and then to who He is. If we are going to rejoice and give thanks in suffering, we must be transformed by the renewing of our minds! Our thoughts about suffering need to change. We need to begin to meditate on the value of suffering and on God's goal in allowing it: to make us a clearer channel of His life and cause us to know him more intimately in the fellowship of His sufferings.

Many of us are familiar with Fanny Crosby's beautiful hymns "Blessed Assurance," "All the Way My Savior Leads Me," and "Near the Cross." These well-loved hymns have been sung by Christians for decades. Fanny Crosby is an excellent example of what it means to rejoice in suffering and to see the power of God manifested in a life.

When Fanny was only six weeks old, she caught a cold and her eyes were affected. A doctor was called, but he prescribed a wrong treatment. Instead of helping her eyes, the poultices he prescribed resulted in permanent damage to Fanny's eyesight. Instead of complaining and giving in to despair because of her blindness, Fanny flourished. She became the author of countless hymns that are still enjoyed today.

One time, someone commented to Fanny that it was too bad God had allowed her to go blind. Fanny quickly responded by saying that if she had been given a choice at birth, she would have asked to be blind. What caused her to make this surprising statement? She said that because she was blind, the first face she would get to see would be the One who died for her.

Fanny's response expresses a heart transformed by the power of Christ. She chose to trust the goodness of God and to live a life of gratefulness instead of complaining. Instead of resisting the difficulty, sorrow, and supposed "hindrance" of blindness, she embraced it wholeheartedly. Her hymns are the expression of a heart of thankfulness, not self-pity or despair. The chorus to one of her most beloved hymns "Blessed Assurance" reads, *"This is my story, this is my song, Praising my Savior all the day long."*

Fanny Crosby's response to suffering was praise. Her focus was not on what she was missing, but on the joy of walking in a relationship with Christ. The result was that she was able to write numerous hymns that have been sung for decades.

Perhaps you and I are facing suffering like Fanny Crosby did. Our suffering may not be blindness, but likely we all are experiencing something that causes us pain. We must learn to glory in our infirmities, as Fanny did, and embrace the suffering. We must give thanks. No matter what you and I are going through, may praise and thanksgiving to God also be our story and our song all day long.

I have personally experienced the blessing of giving thanks in suffering. In the different trials I have faced, when by the Lord's grace I chose to rejoice in the Lord and give thanks in all things, He filled me with His joy. The trials did not suddenly become easy, and there were still times of pain and tears, but God provided His grace to handle the situations He led me through. God will do the same for each of us as we give thanks in all things.

When I have neglected to give thanks for suffering in my life and instead complained, I have experienced discouragement instead of joy. The joy that comes when we embrace suffering, instead of resisting it, no man can take from us. In fact, trials and hardships can become like fuel that, instead of quenching our thanksgiving, remind us to give thanks all the more!

When you and I are faced with suffering, we are once again left with just two choices. We can either reject the suffering and complain, or we can receive that suffering with thanksgiving. If we suffer for the sake of Christ, we can rejoice in the honor of having fellowship with Him in suffering. The suffering is an opportunity to be led into a deeper knowing of Him.

That I may know him, and the power of his resurrection, and the fellowship of his sufferings, being made conformable unto his death; (Philippians 3:10)

I cannot fully explain to you why it is this way, but there is a degree of intimate knowing of God that only comes through the fellowship of His suffering. When we see the valuable riches of intimately knowing God that come through suffering, we begin to understand that suffering, received with thanksgiving, brings joy! Jesus describes this genuine joy by comparing it to what a woman experiences when she is giving birth to a baby.

> A woman when she is in travail hath sorrow, because her hour is come: but as soon as she is delivered of the child, she remembereth no more the anguish, for joy that a man is born into the world. And ye now therefore have sorrow: but I will see you again, and your heart shall rejoice, and your joy no man taketh from you. (John 16:21–22)

When a woman is giving birth, she experiences agonizing pain. Yet she endures that experience no matter how difficult it is. What would cause her to actually embrace pain and agony? She rejoices because of the incredible joy set before her: of holding her newborn baby in her arms. The Lord has a goal in mind when He allows us to suffer: of forming the life of His Son within us. The trials and suffering He brings us through in order to reach that goal are often agonizingly painful, but they are worth it. There is a joy set before us that causes us to give thanks for the suffering. In a sense, the pains of suffering are like the pains of childbirth: they are a necessary part of God's goal being accomplished and are a sign that everything is normal. Paul writes in Galatians 4:19 to the believers: *"My little children, of whom I travail in birth again until Christ be formed in you."* Instead of complaining, let us rejoice in trials, knowing that the Lord who is birthing a good work in us and others is faithful to complete it.

Confirming the souls of the disciples, and exhorting them to continue in the faith, and that we must through much tribulation enter into the kingdom of God. (Acts 14:22)

Maybe you have resisted God's grace and murmured and complained about your circumstances. I urge you to get on your knees before God, confess your ungratefulness, and begin to give thanks in the midst of whatever trial you are facing. God will give you grace and He will sustain you. The Lord truly does all things well!

CHAPTER TEN

THANKSGIVING
AND VICTORY

D<small>ID YOU KNOW</small> that we are currently at war? All believers in the Lord Jesus are soldiers facing an intense spiritual battle. The forces of the world, the flesh, and the devil constantly barrage us with lies and seek to destroy us. There is something gloriously unusual about this battle in which you and I are engaged. The outcome of this war has been decided: Jesus Christ has *already* won the victory!

How did Jesus win the war against the world, the flesh, and the devil? Colossians tells us that Christ won the victory when He died on the cross and nailed to that cross the handwriting of ordinances that was against us. (See Colossians 2:14–15.) It is impossible with mere human words to convey how wonderful this news is—this amazing news that so many are not yet aware of—that *Jesus has already won!*

First, we must understand that we are in a war. Second, we must understand that Christ has won that war. You may be wondering why we are in a war if the war was already won. If the victory over the world, the flesh, and the devil through the power of Christ Jesus has been won, why do we still face spiritual warfare? Why do we struggle to not yield to the flesh? In short, if the war has been won, why do we still face daily battles?

Those questions are deep, yet they are not the most important questions we can ask. Christ has already won. As believers in Christ, you and I are justified and therefore receive, through our oneness with Him, His victory. That is a fact. Instead of asking, "Why is there a battle when Christ has already won?" We should be asking, "Since there is no doubt that Christ has already won, and there is a war being waged on this earth, how can I walk in the victory that Christ already won?" The first question is fraught with doubt; the second question is founded on both the truth of what God has done as well as the reality of the conflict we face.

We also should not be asking how we can win the war, but how to join in Christ's victory. God did not give us the responsibility of winning; He took care of that Himself. He gave us the joyous duty of experiencing the victory that has already been won.

1 Corinthians 15:57 says, *"But thanks be to God, which giveth us the victory through our Lord Jesus Christ."* Psalm 106 gives added insight into how we triumph: we triumph in His praise, in praising the One Who already triumphed. *"Save us, O Lord our God, and gather us from among the heathen, to give thanks unto thy holy name, and to triumph in thy praise"* (Psalm 106:47). It is not a surprise that one of the vital ways to receive the victory of Jesus is through giving thanks.

God has given us His Word and His life. He has given us everything we need to live a victorious Christian life. This includes the armor, the strength, the power, and the light we need, because He has given us *Himself*. If we want to walk in victory, we do not need to desperately seek for victory; we need to receive the victory that has already been won. Instead of flailing like a drowning man without hope, we need to thank God for what He has already provided. We should come to God on the foundation of a completed victory. After all, *"...his divine power hath given unto us all things that pertain unto life and godliness, through the knowledge of him that hath called us to glory and virtue"* (2 Peter 1:3). We can live in freedom from the sins that so easily beset us! Christ has conquered sin! He has given victory over sin when He took us to the cross.

An amazing example of walking in the victory of Jesus Christ in the midst of intense suffering is Corrie ten Boom. She lived with her family in Holland when WWII came tearing through her country. History tells us of many terrible things that happened during that war, including the Holocaust. Thousands of Jews were killed by the Nazis. Corrie ten Boom and her family worked with the Dutch underground resistance to courageously hide Jews from their cruel persecutors. Although they tried their best to remain undetected, Corrie and her family were found and arrested. Many of the family members died in prison or as a result of their time in prison. Eventually, Corrie and her godly sister Betsie were imprisoned in a Nazi concentration camp. This was a time of intense suffering. After Corrie was released from prison, rather than living in bitterness and fear as a result of the suffering she had endured, through the power of Christ, she was able to walk in forgiveness and love. In fact, she later came in contact with one of the cruelest guards from the concentration camp, forgave the man, and remained free from bitterness.

How could Corrie remain thankful, inwardly victorious, and free despite the unimaginable suffering she endured? One incident from her time in prison gives us insight into the answer to this question. Corrie's first day after being moved to the concentration camp was miserable and she was discouraged. She expressed her frustration to Betsie, saying she did not know how she was going to bear being in this new camp and its miserable conditions. Betsie prayed and asked God how they would be able to bear it. Then her eyes lit up. She announced to Corrie that the Lord had already given them the answer in their Bible that morning when they had read 1 Thessalonians 5. Betsie pointed out verse 18: *"In every thing give thanks: for this is the will of God in Christ Jesus concerning you."* She told Corrie that they needed to begin giving thanks.

What, Corrie wondered, could they possibly find to give thanks for in the miserable prison camp? Betsie gave her a list: they should give thanks that they had a Bible. The fact that they were able to sneak a Bible past the guards and into the concentration camp was a miracle! So Corrie and Betsie gave thanks for the Bible. Then Betsie added that they could give thanks for the cramped quarters in the prison camp because this meant that there were many more people with whom they could talk about the Lord and with whom they could hold Bible studies. Corrie and Betsie gave thanks for the cramped quarters.

Then Betsie gave a reason for thanksgiving that Corrie could hardly swallow. Betsie said that they should give thanks *for the fleas!* Give thanks for the fleas? Corrie could understand giving thanks for the Bible and the people, but the fleas? What could possibly be good about thousands of biting, irritating insects that plagued their barracks? Betsie smiled and reminded Corrie that the Lord wanted them to give thanks in all things, not only the things they liked or the things that were easy. So Corrie and Betsie gave thanks for those fleas.

Something about the prison camp they were in puzzled Corrie. The guards almost never came to check the barracks where Corrie and Betsie lived. This allowed them to read their Bible more freely, talk about the Lord with the other women, and hold Bible studies. They were not able to do that in other parts of the prison camp where the guards watched so closely. Corrie didn't understand why the guards gave them such freedom.

One day, when Corrie returned to their bunk, she found Betsie beaming with delight. Betsie found out why the guards did not enter the barracks. They gave Corrie and Betsie's barracks a wide berth for a simple reason: *the fleas!* Corrie was amazed. The Lord truly was working everything together for good. Even an infestation of fleas was God's vehicle to bring about His purpose. Corrie saw the importance of giving thanks in all things, even things that caused her to suffer. I believe that one of the reasons that she was able to remain free from bitterness was because she received the grace of God as she gave thanks in suffering.

If we are going to live in the victory of Christ over complaining and bitterness like Corrie did, we must accept as fact the truth that God already fully accomplished victory in Christ. We must spend time thinking upon and treasuring in our hearts the reality of our victory in Him. If you meditate on the victory that Christ has won on the cross, be forewarned that you will eventually be brought to a place of fully believing this powerful truth and will not be able to stop praising the Lord, even in the midst of suffering and difficulty! *"Then believed they his words; they sang his praise…Save us, O LORD our God, and gather us from among the heathen, to give thanks unto thy holy name, and to triumph in thy praise"* (Psalm 106:12, 47). It is when we believe His Word that we sing His praise. Thanksgiving comes as a result of believing the promises of God.

Do we long for victory in our walk with God—to live victorious over sin, the flesh, and the devil? It is important to remember a very simple and profound truth: to be a conqueror, we must first be conquered; to be an overcomer, we must first be overcome. The only way to live in victory is to be conquered by Christ. It is through death to self that we are filled with the life of Christ. The life of Christ is victory. Our response to this realization must be to give thanks to God Who always causes us to triumph in Christ! All too often we beg God for victory over sin without realizing He already gave us victory by the cross. He desires that we receive it from Him by faith with thanksgiving. It would be reasonable for us therefore to infuse our prayers with thanksgiving!

2 Chronicles 20 contains an amazing example of some men who triumphed through praising the Lord. King Jehoshaphat and the people of Judah were in trouble. Three armies had united together to attack Jehoshaphat and his army, and Judah was severely outnumbered. Jehoshaphat greatly feared this multitude and turned to seek the Lord. The trial Jehoshaphat faced brought him to a place of humility, as trials often do in our lives, and caused him to set himself to seek the Lord. He proclaimed a fast throughout all Judah during this extremely serious situation. (See 2 Chronicles 20:3.)

As a result of the impending enemy attack, the people gathered together to seek the Lord's face and to ask His help. King Jehoshaphat stood in the congregation of Judah and Jerusalem and prayed a powerful prayer in which he appealed to the Lord to help them because of God's covenant with His people. He reminded God of His promises and brought the whole situation before the Lord. He concluded his prayer with the words:

> O our God, wilt thou not judge them? for we have no might against this great company that cometh against us; neither know we what to do: but our eyes are upon thee. (2 Chronicles 20:12)

When I am faced with trials or situations and I do not know what to do, Jehoshaphat's prayer has been in my heart and on my lips: *"Neither know we what to do: but our eyes are upon thee."* When our eyes are fixed on our trials, we tend to worry and become discouraged. When we turn our gaze upon the Lord and keep our focus on Him, even when facing impossible situations, we can be filled with His peace. King Jehoshaphat kept his eyes fixed upon Jehovah, even when he was facing a battle that seemed impossible to the human eye.

After this amazing prayer, the Spirit of the Lord came on a man named Jahaziel. He spoke through Jahaziel to King Jehoshaphat and gave him a heartening message. He promised that the Lord would fight the battle for the people of Judah and give them the victory. Next, He gave them their orders. Their responsibility was simple: to stand still and see the salvation of God.

Ye shall not need to fight in this battle: set yourselves, stand ye still, and see the salvation of the LORD with you, O Judah and Jerusalem: fear not, nor be dismayed; to morrow go out against them: for the LORD will be with you. (2 Chronicles 20:17)

God's call to us is the same as it was to the people of Judah: to stand still and see His salvation instead of being afraid or dismayed. He tells us to go forth to the battle without fear because He is with us. Often, our natural response to the spiritual warfare around and within us is fear. We find ourselves discouraged and falling into failure because we are violating our jurisdiction. As with the children of Israel, our job is not to fight our battles and win them in our own effort and strength; the battle belongs to the Lord. Our jurisdiction is to stand still in Christ, to abide in Him, and to meditate on His Word. Then we will see the salvation of the Lord.

When Jehoshaphat and the people of Judah heard that the Lord would fight for them and give them victory, they fell on their faces before the Lord and worshiped Him. Next, the Levites stood up and began to praise the Lord with a loud voice. They did so because they knew that He had given them the victory. In the same way, we have been given victory because we are abiding in Christ. The Lord has already fought for us! Therefore, we should also praise God with a loud voice.

And they rose early in the morning, and went forth into the wilderness of Tekoa: and as they went forth, Jehoshaphat stood and said, Hear me, O Judah, and ye inhabitants of Jerusalem;

Believe in the LORD your God, so shall ye be established; believe his prophets, so shall ye prosper. (2 Chronicles 20:20)

The next part of this account is astounding. Imagine being one of the people of Judah. You just learned that your country is being attacked by an enemy that far outnumbers your army. Imagine the anxiety and terror that would wash over you when you realize that your foe is not just threatening you; they are endangering the lives of your family and friends. You probably would start right away trying to figure out the best possible battle strategy, hoping desperately to save your life and others' lives. Next, you meet with the king and a group of officers, hoping that together you will come up with a brilliant plan. Your heart is still gripped with fear, however, certain that even the cleverest strategy will not be able to defeat your approaching enemy. You listen as the king announces that a plan has been formed. You lean forward, eager to hear of any ray of hope, any good battle plan. The king begins by saying that he is going to appoint some men to lead the charge. You wonder what maneuvers these men will make. The king goes on to tell you. He describes how the leading group will advance. They will march into battle…singing. *Singing!* You can't believe your ears! The king is facing a massive army far stronger than you, and his only tactical maneuver is singing! Singing is something that an army does *after* the victory has been won, not when victory is farthest from possible! That is precisely why Jehoshaphat implemented the plan as he did; he knew that the Lord would fight for His people and that their victory was already assured.

> And when he had consulted with the people, he
> appointed singers unto the Lord, and that should
> praise the beauty of holiness, as they went out
> before the army, and to say, Praise the Lord; for
> his mercy endureth for ever. (2 Chronicles 20:21)

The men of Judah knew that, for all practical purposes, the battle against their enemies had already been won. The Lord promised that He would fight for them, so their victory was assured, and they marched into battle acting like victors, because they *were* victors already in the Lord.

As believers in the Lord Jesus Christ, you and I also walk as victors. The victory has already been won at the cross! Jesus Christ made open display of the principalities and powers on the cross and triumphed over them. At the same time, the enemy of our souls, Satan, was defeated! The reality is that we are not facing an unlikely victory, or even a merely possible victory. Our victory has without doubt been accomplished. With this confidence we march into battle singing praises and thanking the Lord.

As believers, one of the strongest tactical weapons we have is giving thanks to the Lord and singing His praise. This kind of battle strategy is based on the foundation of the work that Christ has already accomplished, the victory He already won. Marching into battle singing praise to the Lord is part of receiving and participating in His victory. This strategy was formed by God Himself, and it is one vitally important way that God equips us to fight our spiritual enemies. *"For we wrestle not against flesh and blood, but against principalities, against powers, against the rulers of the darkness of this world, against spiritual wickedness in high places"* (Ephesians 6:12). Let us sing praises to the Lord and give thanks to Him, walking and living in the victory over the world, the flesh, and the devil that is ours in Him.

Psalm 149:5–6 gives a stirring battle cry for the spiritual battle we are engaged in: *"Let the saints be joyful in glory: let them sing aloud upon their beds. Let the high praises of God be in their mouth, and a two-edged sword in their hand[.]"* Let us act like the victors that we are in Christ. *"Likewise reckon ye also yourselves to be dead indeed unto sin, but alive unto God through Jesus Christ our Lord"* (Romans 6:11). We *are* dead unto sin, and we *are* alive unto God through Christ. One way we reckon this to be true is through giving thanks.

How did Jehoshaphat and the people of Judah fare in the ensuing battle that they approached with singing? As soon as they began singing, the Lord set ambushes against their enemies. As a result, Judah's enemies destroyed themselves.

> And when they began to sing and to praise, the LORD set ambushments against the children of Ammon, Moab, and mount Seir, which were come against Judah; and they were smitten. For the children of Ammon and Moab stood up against the inhabitants of mount Seir, utterly to slay and destroy them: and when they had made an end of the inhabitants of Seir, every one helped to destroy another. (2 Chronicles 20:22–23)

When they began to sing and praise, the Lord worked mightily to deliver His people from their enemies. As soon as the words of praise came out of their mouths, the enemy

ALWAYS AND IN EVERYTHING

destroyed themselves. By the time the army of Judah arrived on the battlefront, all that was left to do was to gather the spoils of their enemies. The Lord had won the victory for them, just as He had promised.

Scripture says that death and life are in the power of the tongue. When we give thanks and praise the Lord, we are speaking life and victory and proclaiming the kingdom of God. Giving thanks is reckoning that we are more than conquerors in Christ. He fights for us. His victory is ours. Victory over the world, the flesh, and the devil is already accomplished. As we offer the sacrifice of thanksgiving and verbalize praises to our King, like the people of Judah, we see God's promises coming true before our eyes. We can walk in this triumph as we give thanks in all things. *"Now thanks be unto God, which always causeth us to triumph in Christ, and maketh manifest the savour of his knowledge by us in every place"* (2 Corinthians 2:14).

Sometimes we do not understand how we can receive and enjoy the victory that Christ has accomplished on our behalf. How are *we* more than conquerors when *Christ* fought and won the victory? How does giving thanks cause us to join in this victory? Imagine that you have a friend competing in a marathon. Imagine that he invites you to watch him run. You watch your friend throw all his energy into running and finally cross the finish line first in the race with a cry of victory. You cheer wildly and leap out of your seat on the sidelines. You did nothing to earn the victory. You did not spend hours training and working out like your friend did. You did not even run the race yourself. Yet, by cheering for your friend and rejoicing in his victory, you are triumphing in his victory. In a sense, you participated in his triumph and are more than a conqueror. You did not do any work to get the victory, and there is nothing you can do to add to what your friend has accomplished; through cheering and rejoicing with your friend who already won the victory, his triumph became yours.

As believers in Jesus, it is the same for us. Jesus won the victory on the cross. We did nothing to earn this victory. The way we participate in the victory is by rejoicing in it, just as you would take part in your friend's victory by cheering for him. There is nothing we can do to add to Jesus' victory; it is a finished work. We simply need to triumph in it through praising the Lord for winning the victory.

When your friend crossed the finish-line and won the race, if you did not cheer, your friend's victory would not have been diminished at all. He would have still run the race and would still be the true victor; you would have been the one left out. By not cheering for him, you would be choosing not to partake in the victory your friend won. The victory is still a reality, but you would not share it. Do we long to see the victory of Christ in our daily lives? If we are to partake in His victory, we must rejoice in the Lord Jesus Christ.

In Christ, we are more than conquerors. We march into battle singing praises to the Lord Who has already won the victory for us. Let us shout unto God with the voice of triumph! *"O clap your hands, all ye people; shout unto God with the voice of triumph"* (Psalm 47:1). Often when we hear about our victory in Christ, we are quick to think of that victory as a narrow win. We know that the Lord conquered Satan and all his principalities and powers on the cross, but we imagine that it was a close fight in which Christ barely won at the last minute. Christ's victory is not like a basketball game when a buzzer is about to sound and one of the players shoots a ball and barely makes a hoop at the last minute, just narrowly winning the victory. The truth is that Christ did not barely win. God never held His breath wondering what the outcome of the cross would be! Instead, He completely vanquished the enemy with all authority and power.

Christ conquered not only Satan and death; He also conquered me. I am completely crucified with Him on the cross. My desperately wicked flesh has been conquered, through the cross, and now I have been raised to newness of life in Christ. Yes, there is a war going on. It is a war that Christ has won. We are powerless to fight spiritual battles and win them on our own. We must embrace the cross, letting go of our own efforts and pride, and give thanks to Christ for *His* victory. As we march into battle singing to the Lord Whose mercy endures forever, as we leap to our feet, cheering for Christ Who has done it all, we triumph in His praise.

What a wonderful reality this is that God has won the victory and His victory becomes our victory when we thank and praise Him. In God's command to give thanks in everything, He is inviting us to participate in His victory, experience His joy, know constant fellowship with Him, and overcome murmuring and complaining. The journey of learning to give thanks in everything is a wonderful one that the Lord still has me on. May the Lord bless you as you also embark on this exciting journey of learning to praise the Lord in all circumstances. May the Lord take you deeper in your relationship with Him than ever before as you, by His grace, begin to give thanks *always and in everything*.

ABOUT THE AUTHOR

Gabriel Cleator was saved at an early age and raised in a Christian home. Gabriel has a bachelor's degree in biblical ministries and his passion is to encourage believers to go deep in their relationship with the Lord. In his free time, Gabriel enjoys photography, fishing, and visiting national parks. Gabriel and his wife, Sara, live in east Texas, where he serves with a Christian ministry.

CONTACT THE AUTHOR

For questions or comments about this book
or to get in touch with Gabriel Cleator,
please send an email to
rejoiceandgivethanks@gmail.com.
We would love to hear from you!